Unleashing the Willpower Within

A Multidisciplinary Exploration

Mike Feng Zheng

ISBN: 978-1-80128-835-4

Dedication

To my father, Shide Zheng, who taught me to see the world at its full potential.

To my mother, BiYun Wang, who was always more concerned with her children than herself.

To my wife, Ying Chen, who is my support.

To my daughters, Wendy Zheng and Willa Zheng, I am excited to grow alongside you.

Acknowledgment

Unleashing the Willpower Within, like any other book, would not have been able to be written without the assistance of many people who assisted me along the way. There are way too many for this to be a complete list. On the other hand, a select few have been incredibly supportive, including Paul Smith, who assisted me and provided direction throughout the process. Michelle Young is someone who inspires me, directs me, and grounds me. My wife, Ying Chen, and my daughter, Wendy Zheng, are tremendous sources of support and encouragement for me.

About the Author

Mike Feng Zheng is an entrepreneur, financier, and author. He was born in China and moved to the U.S. in 1996. He is interested in writing books in various genres like investment, self-help, and fantasy. He is the author and co-author of several books, including The Art of Money: An Ultimate Guide to Pursuing Prosperity and Happiness, The Money Intelligence, 12 Principles for Life, Ten More Principles for Life, Skullduggery Nightmares, and Whisper in the Storm. Mike Feng Zheng is currently married and the father of two daughters. His older daughter, Wendy, who is ten years old, is also an author. They live in Dallas, TX.

Contents

Chapter 1: The Nature of Willpower

1.1 Defining Willpower

Willpower, also called self-control, self-discipline, or self-regulation, is the ability to control one's thoughts, emotions, impulses, and actions to achieve a desired goal or outcome. This complex mental faculty is essential for making decisions, resisting temptations, and navigating the challenges of modern life. This section will define willpower, delve into some compelling examples and stories, and discuss the scientific research underpinning our understanding of this crucial psychological resource.

In one of the most famous studies on willpower, psychologist Walter Mischel conducted the "Marshmallow Test" in the late 1960s and early 1970s at Stanford University. The experiment involved young children being offered a choice between one marshmallow immediately or two marshmallows if they could wait for a short period, typically 15 minutes. This study demonstrated that delaying gratification and exercising self-control are crucial predictors of success in various aspects of life, including academic achievement, social relationships, and mental health.

The story of Ulysses and the Sirens from Greek mythology also serves as a powerful illustration of willpower. Recognizing the irresistible allure of the

Sirens' song, Ulysses ordered his crew to plug their ears with beeswax and bind him to the mast of the ship. This way, he could hear the enchanting music without succumbing to its deadly temptation. This ancient tale demonstrates the importance of anticipating challenges to our self-control and creating strategies to overcome them.

Another inspiring example of willpower comes from the life of Victor Frankl, a Holocaust survivor and the author of "Man's Search for Meaning." Despite the unimaginable horrors he endured in concentration camps, Frankl relied on his mental fortitude to find meaning and purpose in his suffering. His story is a testament to the power of willpower in the face of adversity and its crucial role in our ability to persevere.

In recent years, scientific research has provided valuable insights into the nature of willpower. A groundbreaking study by psychologist Roy Baumeister and his colleagues found that willpower operates like a muscle, susceptible to fatigue and strengthening through exercise. In a series of experiments, participants who exerted self-control in one task were subsequently more likely to give in to temptation in another task, illustrating the phenomenon of "ego depletion."

However, further research has also revealed that our beliefs about willpower can significantly impact its availability. In a study led by Stanford psychologist Carol Dweck, participants who believed willpower was an unlimited resource were less likely to experience ego depletion than those who viewed it as a finite resource.

Adopting an optimistic mindset about our self-control capacities can help us better navigate situations that require discipline and restraint.

Another intriguing area of research revolves around "grit," a term popularized by psychologist Angela Duckworth. Grit is defined as perseverance and passion for long-term goals, and it is a better predictor of success than intelligence or talent. Cultivating grit involves harnessing our willpower to stay committed to our goals, even when faced with setbacks or obstacles.

The role of habits in willpower cannot be overstated. As renowned psychologist William James once said, "All our life, so far as it has definite form, is but a mass of habits." By developing positive habits, we can conserve our willpower for more challenging tasks, as the automaticity of habits requires less conscious effort to maintain. This idea is supported by research on "keystone habits," foundational routines that can lead to positive changes in various aspects of our lives.

Willpower is also intimately connected to our emotional well-being. Research has shown that individuals with higher levels of self-control tend to experience greater emotional stability and lower levels of anxiety, depression, and stress. Moreover, practicing emotional regulation techniques, such as mindfulness and cognitive reappraisal, can enhance our willpower by helping us to manage difficult emotions more effectively.

The ability to strengthen willpower is not exclusive to adults; research has shown that even young children can improve their self-control through targeted interventions. One study found that when preschoolers were taught strategies for delaying gratification, such as imagining the marshmallow as a picture or a fluffy cloud, they were better able to resist the temptation to eat the treat immediately. This demonstrates that willpower is a malleable skill that can be cultivated and improved throughout our lives.

1.2 The Psychology of Self-Control

The psychology of self-control is a rich and varied field, encompassing numerous theories and perspectives on the nature of willpower. In this section, we will delve into several influential theories supported by compelling examples, data, studies, and surveys to understand willpower's psychological aspects comprehensively.

One of the earliest theories in self-control is Sigmund Freud's psychoanalytic perspective, which posits that willpower arises from the conflict between the id, the ego, and the superego. The id, driven by primal desires, seeks immediate gratification, while the superego represents our moral conscience. The ego mediates between the two, exercising self-control to satisfy the id's desires in socially acceptable ways.

Freud's theory highlights the importance of understanding the unconscious motives that influence our behavior and the role of self-awareness in self-control.

In the 1950s, psychologist Julian Rotter introduced the concept of locus of control, which refers to the extent to which individuals believe they have control over their lives. Those with an internal locus of control perceive that their actions and decisions significantly influence their outcomes. In contrast, those with an external locus attribute their circumstances to external forces or luck. Research has shown that individuals with a strong internal locus of control tend to exhibit greater self-control and are more likely to achieve their goals.

Social cognitive theory, pioneered by psychologist Albert Bandura, emphasizes the role of self-efficacy in self-control. Self-efficacy is the belief in one's ability to accomplish a specific task or achieve a desired outcome. According to this theory, individuals with high self-efficacy are more likely to persevere in the face of obstacles and maintain their self-control. Bandura's famous "Bobo doll" experiment demonstrated the power of observational learning and modeling in shaping self-control and self-efficacy.

The dual-systems theory, known as the "hot and cool" model, offers another perspective on self-control. According to this theory, two distinct cognitive systems drive our behavior: the impulsive, emotion-driven "hot" system and the rational, deliberative "cool" system. Self-control is exercised when the cool system effectively regulates the hot system. This model is supported by research on brain regions such as the prefrontal cortex, which is involved in executive functions like decision-making and impulse control.

In the late 1990s, psychologist Roy Baumeister proposed the strength model of self-control, which posits that willpower is a finite resource that can be depleted through use, a phenomenon known as ego depletion. The famous "radish and chocolate" experiment conducted by Baumeister and his colleagues demonstrated that participants who resisted the temptation to eat chocolate were subsequently less able to persist in a difficult cognitive task, suggesting that their willpower had been depleted.

However, more recent research has challenged the notion of ego depletion, suggesting that the experience of willpower depletion may be influenced by one's beliefs and expectations about self-control resources. A series of studies led by Carol Dweck and Greg Walton found that individuals who believed willpower was an unlimited resource were less likely to experience depletion than those who viewed it as finite.

Another influential theory is Angela Duckworth's concept of grit, which emphasizes the importance of passion and perseverance for long-term goals. Duckworth's research has shown that grit predicts success better than traditional measures such as intelligence or talent.

Her studies on West Point cadets found that those with higher grit levels were more likely to complete the rigorous training program than their less gritty peers.

Mindfulness, a practice rooted in the Buddhist tradition, has also been shown to play a significant role in self-control. By cultivating nonjudgmental awareness of one 's thoughts, emotions, and sensations, mindfulness can help individuals disengage from impulsive behaviors and make more deliberate choices. A study conducted by psychologist Kirk Warren Brown and his colleagues found that individuals with higher levels of mindfulness were better at delaying gratification and exhibited greater self-control.

The role of motivation in self-control has been highlighted by various researchers, including Edward Deci and Richard Ryan, who developed the self-determination theory. According to this theory, intrinsic motivation, which arises from genuine interest and enjoyment, is more conducive to self-control than extrinsic motivation, driven by external rewards or punishments. Supporting this theory, studies have shown that intrinsically motivated individuals exhibit more remarkable persistence and self-control in pursuing their goals.

Another interesting perspective on self-control comes from behavioral economics, which examines the irrational biases and heuristics that influence our decision-making. The concept of "hyperbolic discounting," proposed by economist George Ainslie, posits that individuals tend to disproportionately value immediate rewards over future ones, which can undermine self-control. To counteract this bias, strategies such as precommitment, in which individuals create constraints on their future choices, can be employed to enhance self-control.

Research on habits and their role in self-control has provided valuable insights into how automatic behaviors can influence our ability to exercise willpower. Charles Duhigg, in his book "The Power of Habit," explains that habits are formed through a three-step process: the cue, the routine, and the reward. By understanding and manipulating these components, individuals can create positive habits that support self-control and minimize the need for conscious effort.

In conclusion, the psychology of self-control is a multifaceted field, encompassing a wide range of theories and perspectives that shed light on the complexities of willpower. By examining these various approaches, we can develop a more nuanced understanding of the factors that influence our self-control and the strategies we can employ to enhance it. As we explore the many facets of willpower in the subsequent chapters, we will further uncover the practical implications of these theories and their relevance to our daily lives.

1.3 The Neuroscience of Willpower

The neuroscience of willpower has provided the following:

- A wealth of insights into the biological underpinnings of self-control.
- Revealing the intricate interplay of brain structures.
- Neurotransmitters.
- Hormones that govern our ability to resist temptation and make decisions in line with our long-term goals.

In this section, we will explore some key findings and developments in the neuroscience of willpower, spanning a range of studies and research methodologies.

One of willpower's most critical brain regions is the prefrontal cortex (PFC), which is responsible for executive functions such as decision-making, planning, and impulse control. Research has shown that damage to the PFC can lead to impairments in self-control, as evidenced by the famous case of Phineas Gage, a railroad worker who survived a severe brain injury in the mid-19th century. After the accident, Gage's personality changed dramatically, with a marked decrease in his ability to exercise self-control and make rational decisions.

Functional magnetic resonance imaging (fMRI) studies have further elucidated the role of the PFC in willpower. In a study by researcher Todd Hare and his colleagues, participants were asked to make food choices while their brain activity was monitored. The results revealed that when participants resisted unhealthy food options in favor of healthier ones, the dorsolateral prefrontal cortex (dlPFC), a region associated with self-control, exhibited increased activity.

The anterior cingulate cortex (ACC), another crucial brain region involved in willpower, controls conflict monitoring and error detection. Research has shown that the ACC becomes more active when individuals face situations that require self-control or when they experience cognitive dissonance, reflecting the brain's effort to resolve the conflict between competing desires or beliefs.

The role of dopamine, a neurotransmitter associated with reward and motivation, in willpower, is also significant. Research has shown that dopamine plays a crucial role in the brain's reward system, with higher levels of dopamine being linked to increased motivation and goal-directed behavior. Studies have demonstrated that individuals with a genetic predisposition for higher dopamine levels tend to exhibit greater self-control and persistence in pursuing their goals.

Conversely, low dopamine levels have been associated with impulsivity and poor self-control. For example, research on individuals with attention deficit hyperactivity disorder (ADHD) has revealed that they often have lower dopamine levels, which may contribute to their difficulties with impulse control and focus.

Serotonin, another neurotransmitter, has also been implicated in regulating willpower. Studies have found that low serotonin levels can lead to impulsive behavior and a reduced ability to delay gratification. In one experiment, researchers manipulated serotonin levels in participants through dietary interventions and found that those with lower serotonin levels exhibited more impulsive decision-making.

The hormone cortisol, released in response to stress, has also been shown to influence willpower. Chronic stress can lead to elevated cortisol levels, impairing the PFC's functioning and undermining self-control. This finding highlights the importance of stress management techniques, such as mindfulness and relaxation exercises, in maintaining and enhancing willpower.

The role of glucose in willpower has been a subject of considerable debate in recent years. Early research suggested that glucose was the primary fuel source for self-control. Studies showed that participants who consumed a glucose-rich beverage could better maintain their willpower in subsequent tasks. However, more recent research has challenged this idea, proposing that glucose may not be the sole determinant of willpower and that other factors, such as motivation and mindset, play a significant role.

In addition to these neurochemical factors, research has shown that the brain's plasticity enables individuals to strengthen their willpower over time. Studies on mindfulness and meditation have demonstrated that regular practice can lead to changes in brain structure and function, specifically in regions related to self-control and emotional regulation. For example, a study by neuroscientist Sara Lazar found that long-term meditators had increased gray matter density in the PFC and ACC, suggesting that meditation may enhance willpower by promoting neural growth and connectivity in these critical areas.

Sleep is also a crucial factor in the brain's self-control mechanisms. Research has demonstrated that sleep deprivation can impair the PFC's ability to regulate emotions and impulses effectively, leading to decreased willpower. In a study conducted by Matthew Walker and his colleagues, sleep-deprived participants showed reduced activity in the dlPFC and increased activity in the amygdala, a brain region associated with emotional reactivity, when presented with emotionally charged images. This finding underscores the importance of adequate sleep for maintaining optimal self-control.

The impact of exercise on willpower is another area of interest in neuroscience. Research has shown that regular physical activity can lead to changes in the brain that promote self-control and cognitive function. In one study, researchers found that after just a few months of regular aerobic exercise, participants exhibited increased PFC and ACC activity during tasks requiring self-control. Regular physical activity may help strengthen the neural pathways that support willpower.

Understanding the interplay between genetics and environmental factors in the development of willpower is also an important area of research. Twin studies have indicated that self-control has a significant heritable component, with genetic factors accounting for approximately 50% of the variation in self-control among individuals. However, environmental factors, such as parenting styles and early life experiences, also play a critical role in shaping an individual's capacity for self-control. This underscores the importance of both nature and nurture in developing willpower.

In conclusion, the neuroscience of willpower is a rapidly evolving field that has provided invaluable insights into the biological mechanisms underlying self-control. By examining the intricate interplay of brain structures, neurotransmitters, hormones, and environmental factors, we can better understand the determinants of willpower and devise targeted interventions to enhance this essential psychological resource. As we explore the various aspects of willpower in the subsequent chapters, we will delve further into the practical applications of these findings and their relevance to our daily lives.

Chapter 2: Willpower in History and Philosophy

2.1 Ancient Perspectives on Willpower

This section will explore the ancient perspectives on willpower, delving into the rich history and philosophy of self-control across various civilizations and schools of thought. Understanding how our ancestors grappled with the concept of willpower can provide us with valuable insights and context and inform our modern understanding of this essential human capacity.

The ancient Greeks were among the first to consider willpower and self-control critical virtues. In Greek philosophy, "sophrosyne" describes a sense of self-restraint, moderation, and temperance. This virtue was highly valued by philosophers like Socrates, Plato, and Aristotle, who believed exercising self-control was necessary for achieving personal excellence and happiness, known as "eudaimonia."

In the Platonic tradition, willpower was closely linked to reason and the pursuit of knowledge. Plato's famous allegory of the chariot from his dialogue "Phaedrus" illustrates this idea. The chariot, driven by a charioteer, is pulled by two horses, one representing noble desires and the other representing base desires. The charioteer's task is to control the horses and guide the chariot toward the truth, symbolizing the importance of self-control in achieving wisdom.

In his work "Nicomachean Ethics," Aristotle discussed the concept of "akrasia," or weakness of the will, which occurs when an individual's actions are at odds with their rational judgment. He argued that self-control is necessary to overcome akrasia and that cultivating virtues such as courage and temperance can help individuals align their actions with a rational understanding of what is good.

The Stoic philosophers of ancient Rome also emphasized willpower and self-control. They believed that by cultivating self-mastery, individuals could develop inner tranquility and resilience in the face of external circumstances. Epictetus, a prominent Stoic philosopher, emphasized the importance of focusing on the aspects of life within our control and cultivating a sense of detachment from external events and desires.

In ancient India, the concept of willpower was deeply embedded in the teachings of Hinduism, Buddhism, and Jainism. In Hindu philosophy, the concept of "dharma" or duty, emphasizes the importance of self-control and discipline in fulfilling one's obligations and pursuing spiritual growth. The Bhagavad Gita, a sacred Hindu text, highlights the significance of self-mastery in achieving spiritual enlightenment and inner peace.

The Buddha's teachings in the Pali Canon, a foundational text of Theravada Buddhism, also emphasize the importance of willpower and self-control. The Noble Eightfold Path, which outlines the path to spiritual awakening, includes elements such as "right effort" and "right mindfulness," requiring self-discipline and self-mastery.

Jainism, another ancient Indian religion, strongly emphasizes self-control and asceticism as a means of spiritual purification and liberation. Jain practitioners often engage in rigorous practices of self-discipline, such as fasting, meditation, and physical austerities, to develop their willpower and overcome attachments to the material world.

In ancient China, Confucianism and Daoism both acknowledged the importance of willpower and self-control. Confucius emphasized the cultivation of virtues such as "li" (ritual propriety) and "ren" (benevolence), which require self-discipline and restraint in one's thoughts and actions. On the other hand, Daoism advocated for a more naturalistic approach to self-mastery, emphasizing the importance of aligning one's actions with the natural flow of the universe, known as the "Dao."

These ancient perspectives on willpower provide us with a rich historical and philosophical context for understanding the development of self-control throughout human history. They reveal that, despite the differences in cultural and religious beliefs, the importance of willpower and self-discipline has been a recurring theme across civilizations.

In ancient Persia, Zoroastrianism, one of the world's oldest monotheistic religions, also stressed the importance of self-control and the struggle between good and evil within the individual. Zoroastrian teachings emphasize the need for humans to exercise their free will in choosing to act by the principles of "asha" (truth, order, and righteousness) and resist the temptations of "druj" (deceit and chaos). This internal struggle requires the cultivation of willpower and moral integrity.

While not explicitly discussing willpower as a concept, the ancient Egyptian civilization also emphasized self-control and moral behavior. In their belief system, the afterlife judgment of an individual's soul was based on weighing their heart against the feather of Ma'at, the goddess of truth, justice, and harmony. Living life by Ma'at's principles required self-discipline and restraint in one's actions.

The Islamic tradition, which emerged in the 7th century C.E., similarly emphasizes the significance of self-control and discipline, particularly in spiritual practice. "jihad al-nafs," or the struggle against one's ego and base desires, is a central aspect of Islamic spirituality. Practicing self-control in the form of fasting during the holy month of Ramadan is one of the Five Pillars of Islam and serves as a means of fostering self-discipline and spiritual growth.

In the Jewish tradition, the concept of "yetzer hara" (the evil inclination) and "yetzer hatov" (the good inclination) represents the internal struggle between an individual's base desires and moral preferences. Jewish teachings emphasize the importance of self-control in overcoming the yetzer hara and living a righteous life by the commandments of the Torah.

The Christian tradition also recognizes the significance of willpower and self-control in the context of spiritual growth and moral behavior. The Apostle Paul, in his letters to the early Christian communities, frequently discussed the struggle between the "flesh" and the "spirit" and emphasized the importance of self-control as a virtue and a fruit of the Holy Spirit.

In summary, the ancient perspectives on willpower and self-control offer a fascinating glimpse into the universal human struggle to achieve self-mastery and moral integrity. Across cultures and religious traditions, cultivating willpower has been recognized as a crucial aspect of personal development and spiritual growth. These historical insights serve as a foundation for our modern understanding of willpower and provide a rich context for further exploration of this essential human capacity in the subsequent chapters.

2.2 The Enlightenment and the Emergence of the Will

The Enlightenment, a cultural and intellectual movement that emerged in Europe during the 17th and 18th centuries, brought about a significant shift in understanding human nature, including the concept of willpower—this period, characterized by an emphasis on reason, scientific inquiry, and individualism, led to new theories about the nature of the human will and its role in shaping human behavior.

One of the key figures of the Enlightenment, the French philosopher René Descartes, contributed to the development of the modern concept of the will through his influential works on mind-body dualism. Descartes argued that the mind and the body are distinct entities, with the mind possessing the capacity for rational thought and free will. In his view, the will was an essential aspect of the human mind, responsible for making choices and directing human action.

In contrast to Descartes' dualistic view, the British philosopher Thomas Hobbes espoused a materialistic understanding of human nature. Hobbes believed that human behavior was determined by a complex interplay of desires and aversions, referred to as "appetites" and "aversions." According to Hobbes, the human will result from these competing internal forces, with actions determined by whichever force is strongest at a given moment.

Another Enlightenment philosopher, John Locke, further developed the concept of the will in his work "An Essay Concerning Human Understanding." Locke argued that the will is not a distinct faculty of the mind but rather an expression of an individual's desires and preferences. In his view, human action is determined by the balance of competing desires, with the will acting as a mechanism for selecting and pursuing the most pressing desire.

David Hume, a Scottish philosopher and key figure of the Enlightenment, offered a different perspective on the nature of the will. Hume was skeptical of a distinct faculty of the will, instead arguing that a combination of reason and passion drives human actions. According to Hume, reason alone cannot motivate action; passions or emotions drive human behavior. In Hume's view, the will is merely the capacity to act according to one's strongest passions.

In his seminal work "Critique of Pure Reason," the German philosopher Immanuel Kant developed a more nuanced understanding of the will, which he referred to as the "faculty of desire." Kant distinguished between "pathological" desires, which are influenced by external factors and inclinations, and the "rational" desires, which are determined by the moral law. According to Kant, exercising free will involves acting according to the moral law, independent of one's pathological desires.

Kant's concept of the will is closely linked to his ethical theory, known as the "categorical imperative." The categorical imperative is a moral principle that requires individuals to act according to maxims that could be universally applied without contradiction. In this framework, the exercise of willpower involves making choices consistent with the categorical imperative, regardless of one's inclinations or desires.

The Enlightenment also saw the emergence of utilitarianism, an ethical theory that evaluates actions based on their consequences. Utilitarian philosophers, such as Jeremy Bentham and John Stuart Mill, argued that human actions should be guided by the principle of "the greatest happiness for the greatest number." In this framework, the will is the capacity to make choices that maximize overall happiness and minimize suffering.

During the Enlightenment, the concept of the will also became intertwined with political theory and the development of modern democracy. The French philosopher Jean-Jacques Rousseau, in his work "The Social Contract," argued that the will of the people, or the "general will," should be the basis for political decision-making and the foundation of legitimate government.

Rousseau's ideas on the general will influenced the development of democratic principles and the notion that political power should derive from the collective will of the citizenry.

In economics, the Scottish philosopher and economist Adam Smith also touched upon the will concept in his landmark work, "The Wealth of Nations." Smith's theory of the "invisible hand" posited that individuals, acting in their self-interest and guided by their wills, inadvertently contribute to the overall welfare of society. Smith's ideas laid the groundwork for modern economic theory and highlighted the role of the individual will in shaping market forces and social outcomes.

The will concept was also explored throughout the Enlightenment in literature and the arts. The Romantic movement, which emerged in response to the Enlightenment's emphasis on reason and rationality, celebrated the power of the individual will and its capacity to shape human destiny. Literary works of the period, such as Johann Wolfgang von Goethe's "Faust" and Mary Shelley's "Frankenstein," grappled with themes of free will, personal responsibility, and the consequences of human ambition.

In addition to the contributions of philosophers, writers, and artists, the concept of the will was also influenced by the scientific developments of the time. The Enlightenment marked a period of rapid advancements in fields such as anatomy, physiology, and psychology, which prompted new theories about the relationship between the mind, the body, and human behavior. These scientific discoveries laid the groundwork for the modern study of willpower as researchers began investigating self-control's biological and neurological underpinnings.

As the Enlightenment drew to a close, the concept of the will had become a central aspect of Western thought, with far-reaching implications for philosophy, psychology, political theory, and the arts. The ideas and approaches that emerged during this period continue to shape our understanding of willpower and self-control today, providing a rich foundation for further exploration and inquiry.

In conclusion, the Enlightenment was a pivotal period in developing the modern concept of the will, as philosophers, scientists, and artists sought to understand the nature of human agency and self-control. The ideas and theories that emerged during this time continue to influence our understanding of willpower, providing a vital historical context for contemporary debates and research on the topic. By examining the contributions of key figures such as

Descartes, Hobbes, Locke, Hume, Kant, Rousseau, and Smith, we can gain a deeper appreciation of the complex and multifaceted nature of the will and its role in shaping human behavior and society.

2.3 Willpower in the Modern Era: Psychology, Neuroscience, and Beyond

The modern era has seen significant advancements in our understanding of willpower and self-control, with contributions from various fields of study, including psychology, neuroscience, and behavioral economics. This section will provide an overview of key developments in these areas, offering a comprehensive look at how our understanding of willpower has evolved over the past century.

One of the earliest and most influential psychological theories of willpower emerged in the late 19th and early 20th centuries with the work of Sigmund Freud. Freud's psychoanalytic theory posited the existence of three components of the human psyche: the id, the ego, and the superego. According to Freud, the ego serves as the mediator between the id's instinctual desires and the superego's moral constraints, with willpower arising from the ego's attempts to balance these competing demands.

The behaviorist movement, which gained prominence in the early 20th century, shifted the focus away from the reflective study of the mind and toward the observable aspects of human behavior—influential behaviorist psychologists, such as John B. Watson and B.F. Skinner argued that human actions are primarily determined by environmental factors and conditioning processes. From a behaviorist perspective, willpower could be seen as a learned response to stimuli rather than an inherent aspect of the human psyche.

In the mid-20th century, the cognitive revolution in psychology led to a renewed interest in studying mental processes, including the mechanisms underlying willpower and self-control. Albert Bandura's social cognitive theory, for example, emphasized the importance of self-efficacy, or an individual's belief in their ability to control their behavior, in determining the success of self-regulation efforts.

Another influential cognitive psychologist, Walter Mischel, conducted a series of studies in the 1960s and 1970s that led to the development of the "marshmallow test." This experiment, which measured children's ability to delay gratification to receive a larger reward later, provided valuable insights into the nature of self-control and its long-term effects on success and well-being. Mischel's work laid the groundwork for numerous subsequent studies on cognitive and developmental aspects of willpower.

Neuroscience has also contributed significantly to our understanding of willpower and self-control in recent decades. Neuroscientists have identified key brain regions, such as the prefrontal cortex, that regulate impulses and decision-making processes. Advances in neuroimaging techniques, such as functional magnetic resonance imaging (fMRI), have allowed researchers to investigate the neural correlates of willpower in real-time, providing valuable insights into the biological basis of self-control.

One influential theory that has emerged from the intersection of psychology and neuroscience is the "limited resource" model of willpower, proposed by Roy Baumeister and his colleagues. This model posits that willpower is a finite resource that can be depleted through the exertion of self-control, leading to a state of "ego depletion." The limited resource model has been the subject of extensive research and debate, with some studies supporting the theory and others questioning its validity.

The field of behavioral economics has also made significant contributions to our understanding of willpower by examining how human decision-making deviates from rational models of behavior. For example, Nobel Prize-winning economist Daniel

Kahneman's work on cognitive biases and heuristics has shed light on the mental shortcuts and irrational tendencies that can interfere with self-control and lead to suboptimal choices.

Building on this foundation, Richard Thaler and Cass Sunstein developed the concept of "nudge theory," which explores how subtle changes in the presentation of options can influence decision-making and promote healthier or more responsible choices. Nudge theory has been applied in various contexts, from public policy to personal finance, demonstrating the potential for harnessing insights about human behavior and willpower to improve individual and societal outcomes.

In addition to these interdisciplinary contributions, research on willpower has also been informed by studying individual differences and the factors influencing self-control across different populations. Studies on the role of genetics, for example, have identified heritable components that contribute to variation in willpower and self-regulation. Environmental factors, such as upbringing and social context, have also been shown to play a significant role in shaping an individual's capacity for self-control.

Another area of research that has deepened our understanding of willpower is the study of mindfulness and meditation. Emerging evidence suggests that mindfulness practices, which involve cultivating non-judgmental awareness of one's thoughts and experiences, can enhance self-regulation and improve willpower. Research on the neurological effects of meditation has shown that regular practice can lead to changes in brain structure and function that support self-control, further highlighting the potential for mindfulness techniques to enhance willpower.

In recent years, the field of positive psychology, which focuses on the study of human flourishing and well-being, has also contributed to our understanding of willpower. Research in this area has highlighted the importance of character strengths, such as grit, perseverance, and self-control, in promoting success and happiness. This work has led to the development of interventions and educational programs to foster these strengths and enhance individuals' capacity for self-regulation.

The modern era has witnessed significant advancements in our understanding of willpower, with contributions from diverse fields of study, such as psychology, neuroscience, behavioral economics, and positive psychology. These insights have deepened our knowledge of the complex interplay between biological, cognitive, environmental, and cultural factors that shape human self-control and have paved the way for innovative approaches to enhancing willpower and promoting well-being. By examining these developments and the ongoing research in this area, we can continue to build a comprehensive understanding of willpower and its role in shaping human behavior and outcomes.

Chapter 3: Willpower in Cognitive

3.1 Science The Role of Executive Functions

Executive functioning is a higher-order cognitive process that enables individuals to plan, organize, initiate, and monitor goal-directed behaviors. These functions, primarily regulated by the brain's prefrontal cortex, include working memory, cognitive flexibility, inhibitory control, and metacognitive skills. Together, these processes help us navigate the complexities of daily life, make informed decisions, adapt to changing circumstances, and regulate our emotions and impulses to pursue our goals.

Emily was a bright, ambitious, and hardworking individual who had recently graduated from university and landed her dream job at a prestigious advertising firm. Although Emily was highly talented and driven, she faced unique challenges in her personal and professional life. These challenges are a compelling illustration of executive functions' critical role in our daily lives.

In her first month at the advertising firm, Emily was tasked with developing a creative campaign for one of the company's largest clients. This high-pressure assignment required Emily to juggle multiple responsibilities, from brainstorming innovative ideas to managing tight deadlines and coordinating with various team members. As Emily navigated these complex demands, she relied heavily on her executive functions – the cognitive processes responsible for planning, organizing, initiating, and monitoring goal-directed behaviors.

One day, while Emily worked hard on her campaign, she received a call from her mother, Elizabeth Thompson. Elizabeth was organizing a surprise birthday party for Emily's younger brother, Matthew, and needed Emily's help planning. Eager to contribute, Emily agreed to take on several tasks, such as creating the invitations, coordinating the catering, and planning the entertainment. These new responsibilities added to Emily's full plate, further testing her executive functions.

As the days passed, Emily's reliance on her executive functions became increasingly apparent. She constantly shifted between her work and personal commitments, using her working memory to keep track of important details and deadlines. She also utilized her cognitive flexibility to adapt to unexpected changes, such as last-minute advertising campaign revisions or party plans.

At times, Emily struggled to maintain her focus and motivation, particularly when faced with competing priorities or difficult decisions. In these moments, she relied on her inhibitory control – the ability to suppress distracting thoughts, impulses, or emotions in favor of goal-directed actions. For example, when Emily felt overwhelmed by her workload, she would remind herself of her goals and the importance of her tasks, using her self-discipline to stay on track.

One afternoon, Emily was presented with a particularly challenging situation. Her boss, Jonathan Carter, requested that she attend an urgent meeting with the client, which conflicted with her scheduled time to pick up the catering for Matthew's party. Faced with this dilemma, Emily drew upon her problem-solving skills, another critical component of executive functioning. She quickly evaluated her options and devised a plan, asking her friend and coworker, Sarah Martinez, to attend the meeting on her behalf while she took care of the catering.

As the advertising campaign deadline and Matthew's party date approached, Emily's executive functions were put to the ultimate test. She worked late into the night, carefully reviewing her work and making final adjustments to ensure everything was perfect. This process required Emily to exercise her metacognitive skills or the ability to think about her thinking, as she assessed her progress and identified areas for improvement.

Finally, the big day arrived. Emily presented her completed campaign to Jonathan Carter and the client, who were both thoroughly impressed with her creativity, attention to detail, and ability to deliver under pressure. That evening, Emily attended Matthew's surprise birthday party, where her family and friends marveled at the fantastic event she had helped to orchestrate.

As Emily reflected on her recent experiences, she realized how crucial her executive functions had been in helping her navigate the challenges and complexities of her personal and professional life. She also recognized the importance of developing and strengthening these cognitive skills, as they would undoubtedly serve her well in the future.

In conclusion, the story of Emily Thompson demonstrates the essential role that executive functions play in our daily lives. From planning and organizing to problem-solving and self-regulation, these cognitive processes enable us to navigate the complexities of our personal and professional worlds. By examining Emily's experiences, we can better understand the various components of executive functioning, including working memory, cognitive flexibility, inhibitory control, and metacognitive skills.

Moreover, Emily's story highlights the importance of nurturing and developing these executive functions. As we face new challenges and opportunities, our capacity for self-control, adaptability, and goal-directed behavior can profoundly impact our success and well-being.

The tale of Emily Thompson also serves as a reminder of the interdependence of our executive functions and the need to strike a balance between them. Just as Emily relied on a combination of skills to navigate her professional and personal responsibilities, so must we cultivate a well-rounded set of executive functions to achieve our goals and fulfill our potential.

Finally, Emily's story underscores the potential for growth and improvement in our executive functioning. By recognizing the areas in which we excel and those in which we may struggle, we can strengthen our cognitive skills and enhance our overall performance.

In summary, the story of Emily Thompson provides a vivid illustration of the vital role executive functions play in our lives, offering valuable insights into how these cognitive processes shape our behavior, decision-making, and overall success. By examining Emily's experiences and reflecting on our executive functioning, we can gain a greater appreciation for the importance of these skills and the need to nurture and develop them throughout our lives continually.

3.2 Attention and Focus

Attention refers to the cognitive process of selectively concentrating on a specific aspect of information, whether an external stimulus or an internal thought, while ignoring other irrelevant information. Conversely, the focus is the sustained attention and mental effort directed toward a particular task or goal. Both awareness and focus are crucial for learning, problem-solving, and accomplishing tasks efficiently.

Once in the peaceful town of Willowbrook lived a dedicated high school student named Olivia Johnson. Olivia had always been a diligent student, but as she entered her senior year, she faced numerous distractions and challenges that threatened her ability to concentrate on her studies and maintain her excellent academic record.

One fateful Monday morning, Olivia received a group text message from her best friends, Sophia Williams and Lily Thompson, inviting her to join the school's drama club. Although Olivia was intrigued by the idea of participating in the school play, she knew that joining the club would require a significant time commitment, potentially impacting her ability to focus on her studies.

Determined to strike a balance between her academic pursuits and her social life, Olivia decided to develop a strategy for maintaining her attention and focus. She established a quiet study space in her room, free from distractions like her phone, television, and noisy family members. This dedicated workspace would serve as a haven for concentration and productivity.

As the weeks passed, Olivia found that her newfound study environment helped her maintain her attention and focus during her homework and exam preparation sessions. However, she soon realized that more than a quiet space was needed to ensure her success. She needed to develop additional strategies to improve her concentration and stay on track.

One day, while browsing the internet for tips on enhancing focus, Olivia came across the concept of the Pomodoro Technique. This time management method involved breaking work into short, focused intervals, typically 25 minutes, followed by a brief break. Intrigued, Olivia decided to give the Pomodoro Technique a try during her next study session.

To her delight, Olivia found that the Pomodoro Technique significantly improved her ability to concentrate on her schoolwork. By breaking her tasks into smaller, more manageable chunks, she could maintain her focus and avoid becoming overwhelmed by the sheer volume of work she needed to complete.

In addition to the Pomodoro Technique, Olivia also experimented with mindfulness meditation. This practice involved focusing her attention on her breath and bringing her mind back to the present moment whenever it wandered. Olivia discovered that just a few minutes of mindfulness meditation each day helped sharpen her focus and reduce stress and anxiety.

As the school year progressed, Olivia continued to refine her attention and focus strategies, finding the right balance between her academic responsibilities and her newfound love for the drama club. She found herself excelling in her classes and enjoying her time on stage, as her role in the school play allowed her to channel her creativity and passion.

Ultimately, Olivia's hard work and dedication to improving her attention and focus paid off. She maintained her excellent academic record and even earned a leading role in the school play, much to the delight of her friends, family, and teachers.

Olivia Johnson's story is a powerful illustration of the importance of attention and focuses in our lives. By recognizing the challenges and distractions that hinder our ability to concentrate, we can develop strategies and practices to enhance our focus and focus on the tasks that matter most. Furthermore, Olivia's journey highlights the potential for growth and improvement in our attention and focus, demonstrating that we can overcome obstacles and achieve our goals with determination and effort.

Olivia's experience also highlights the value of exploring and experimenting with different techniques and practices to improve our attention and focus. By adopting strategies such as the Pomodoro Technique, creating dedicated study space, and engaging in mindfulness meditation, we can discover the best methods for us and cultivate our ability to concentrate on our goals.

Moreover, the tale of Olivia Johnson serves as a reminder that maintaining a balance between our personal, academic, and professional commitments is critical for overall well-being. By managing our time and focusing our attention effectively, we can succeed in multiple areas of our lives without becoming overwhelmed or burnt out.

Finally, Olivia's story emphasizes the importance of perseverance and self-awareness in pursuing improved attention and focus. By acknowledging our weaknesses and areas for growth, we can take the necessary steps to develop our cognitive skills and enhance our overall performance.

3.3 Memory and Decision-Making

Memory is the cognitive process of encoding, storing, and retrieving information, while decision-making involves the mental process of selecting a course of action from multiple alternatives. Both memory and decision-making are closely intertwined, as our memories provide the foundation upon which we make choices and judgments.

In the bustling metropolis of River City, there lived a group of close-knit friends: Ava Baker, Ethan Smith, Mia Davis, and Noah Wilson. The four friends had been inseparable since childhood, sharing countless memories and experiences. As they grew older and faced increasingly complex decisions, their memories would play a crucial role in shaping their choices and determining their paths in life.

One summer afternoon, the friends gathered at their favorite café to discuss their plans for the future. With college just around the corner, each faced important decisions about which schools to attend and what majors to pursue.

Ava had always been passionate about the environment and had fond memories of participating in local clean-up initiatives and environmental campaigns. She recalled her excitement when first learning about climate change and renewable energy during a high school science class. Drawing from these memories, Ava decided to pursue a degree in environmental science to continue her efforts in protecting the planet.

On the other hand, Ethan had been captivated by the world of technology since he was a young boy. He remembered the countless hours he spent disassembling and reassembling his father's old computer and the exhilaration of building his first website. These memories helped Ethan decide to pursue a career in computer science, where he could combine his love for technology with his natural problem-solving abilities.

Mia's memories were filled with her love for the arts, particularly the joy she experienced while performing in school plays and attending local theater productions with her friends. Reflecting on these cherished memories, Mia decided to follow her passion and study theater arts in college, hoping to become a professional actress one day.

Noah's decision-making process was more complex as he needed help to choose between his interest in psychology and his writing talent. He thought back to his experiences in high school – the fascinating psychology courses that piqued his curiosity and the thrill of seeing his work published in the school newspaper. Ultimately, Noah decided to major in psychology while continuing to nurture his love for writing through extracurricular activities.

As the friends shared their plans, they found solace in their decisions rooted in the memories that shaped their identities and interests. They felt a sense of confidence in their choices, knowing that they were pursuing their true passions.

Months later, the friends were scattered across the country, each attending a different university. They kept in touch through regular video calls, during which they shared their experiences and offered support to one another as they navigated the challenges of college life.

Ava found herself thriving in her environmental science courses, her passion for the subject fueled by the memories of her past involvement in environmental causes. She eagerly shared her newfound knowledge with her friends and even inspired them to adopt more sustainable practices in their daily lives.

Meanwhile, Ethan dove headfirst into computer science, tackling complex coding challenges and developing innovative software solutions. He often reflected on his childhood memories of tinkering with computers, which constantly reminded him of his love for technology and his desire to make a difference in the field.

Mia's decision to study theater arts proved the right choice, as she flourished on stage and honed her acting skills. She cherished the memories of her first performances and used them as motivation to continue pursuing her dream of becoming a professional actress. As for Noah, his decision to major in psychology allowed him to explore the intricacies of human behavior and mental processes while providing ample opportunities to refine his writing skills. He found that his studies in psychology informed his writing in surprising ways, allowing him to create more nuanced and engaging narratives.

As the years passed, the friends continued to rely on their memories and past experiences to guide their decisions. They each faced various obstacles and opportunities, from internships and job offers to relationships and personal growth.

Ava's commitment to environmental conservation led her to join an influential non-profit organization, where she played a pivotal role in developing policies and initiatives to combat climate change. Her memories of local clean-up efforts and environmental campaigns fueled her passion for making a difference on a global scale.

Ethan's expertise in computer science landed him a job at a prestigious tech company, where he worked on cutting-edge projects that revolutionized the industry. He often thought back to the days when he disassembled his father's computer, marveling at his progress since then. Mia's dedication to her craft paid off, as she eventually landed roles in prominent theater productions and even a few films. Her memories of performing in school plays and attending local theater events served as a reminder of how far she had come and the importance of staying true to her passion.

Noah's decision to study psychology led to a rewarding career as a therapist, where he helped clients navigate the complexities of their emotions and relationships. He also continued to write, eventually publishing a collection of short stories inspired by his experiences and the psychological insights he gained throughout his education.

As the friends gathered for a reunion in River City, they reminisced about their shared past and the memories that had shaped their decisions and, ultimately, their lives. They realized that their memories had influenced their choices and played a crucial role in maintaining their bond and connection over the years.

In conclusion, the story of Ava, Ethan, Mia, and Noah illustrates the powerful interplay between memory and decision-making in our lives. Their experiences demonstrate how memories inform our choices and serve as a foundation for our passions, interests, and identities. Furthermore, the friends' journey highlights the importance of reflecting on our memories and using them as a guide to making informed, authentic decisions that align with our true selves.

Chapter 4: The Biology of Willpower

4.1 Brain Structures and Willpower

Understanding the biology of willpower involves examining the brain structures that play a crucial role in our ability to exercise self-control, resist temptation, and persevere in the face of challenges. Among these structures, the prefrontal cortex is particularly important, as it is responsible for executive functions such as planning, decision-making, and impulse control. Other brain regions, like the anterior cingulate cortex and the striatum, also contribute to our capacity for willpower by regulating attention, motivation, and emotional responses.

The life of renowned physicist Stephen Hawking is an inspiring example of the dynamic interplay between brain structure and willpower. Hawking defied the odds and continued to make seminal contributions to theoretical physics for several decades after being diagnosed with amyotrophic lateral sclerosis (ALS) at 21 and given only a few years to live.

The disease eventually rendered Hawking nearly wholly paralyzed, losing control of his muscles over time. However, he could keep working and maintain his prolific career because his mental faculties were unaffected. The robustness of Hawking's brain's executive functioning systems contributed to his extraordinary willpower.

Hawking's resilience came mainly from his prefrontal cortex, the part of the brain that helps with planning and organization. Despite the physical restrictions imposed by his condition, he could keep his focus and allocate his mental resources well, thanks to this area of the brain.

The anterior cingulate cortex also significantly influenced Hawking's extraordinary resolve. The ability to focus on his work and stay calm despite his many challenges likely stems from activity in a part of the brain responsible for regulating attention and handling conflicting information.

Hawking's willpower was primarily supported by the striatum, a region of the brain associated with motivation and reward. This framework helped him stay interested in physics and feel proud of his accomplishments, which kept him going even when faced with insurmountable obstacles.

The strength of the human mind and its ability to exert will are on display in Hawking's dogged pursuit of scientific knowledge. His story of triumph over adversity provides instructive evidence for the importance of neural circuitry in developing human willpower and tenacity.

In addition to these fundamental brain structures, other factors, such as Hawking's emotional resilience and strong support network, contributed to his extraordinary willpower. His optimistic outlook and single-minded pursuit of his goals despite his handicap indicate the human will's strength and the human brain's adaptability.

The role of encouragement from others and favorable circumstances in developing personal resolve is another theme that emerges from Hawking's life story. Friends, family, and coworkers supported and helped him, contributing to his dogged persistence and eventual success.

In addition, Hawking's success demonstrates that it is possible to develop and strengthen one's resolve, even in the face of formidable challenges. We can build the fortitude and perseverance to realize our ambitions by tapping into the potential of our neural circuitry and surrounding ourselves with positive people and resources.

Finally, the life of Stephen Hawking is a compelling illustration of how neural architecture interacts with resolve. His extraordinary achievements, achieved despite severe physical impairments, shed light on the function of the brain's prefrontal cortex, anterior cingulate cortex, and striatum in these traits.

Furthermore, Hawking's experience emphasizes the significance of a positive outlook, social support, and emotional resilience in developing willpower and completing complicated tasks.

The biological basis of self-control and determination can be better understood by looking at Stephen Hawking's life and the brain structures that contributed to his extraordinary willpower. This insight can then be used to devise measures and interventions that strengthen individual resolve and increase the likelihood of success in the face of adversity.

As we seek further to understand the relationship between brain structures and willpower, it is crucial to recognize that these structures do not work in isolation. Instead, they function as part of a complex, interconnected network that enables us to exert self-control, maintain focus, and persevere in adversity. Understanding the dynamics of this network can provide valuable insights into the mechanisms underlying willpower and inform strategies to enhance our capacity for self-discipline.

One approach to deepening our understanding of the brain and willpower is to investigate the plasticity of these brain structures. Neuroplasticity, the brain's ability to change and adapt in response to experiences and challenges, is a key factor in developing and maintaining willpower. By examining how the prefrontal cortex, anterior cingulate cortex, and striatum change over time as we engage in activities that require self-control, we can gain insights into the potential for growth and improvement in our willpower. This knowledge can then inform interventions and techniques designed to strengthen these brain structures and enhance our capacity for self-discipline and determination.

Another important consideration in studying brain structures and willpower is the role of individual differences. Each person's brain is unique, and factors such as genetics, early life experiences, and environmental influences can shape the development and function of the brain structures involved in willpower. By exploring how these individual differences impact our capacity for self-control, we can better understand the wide range of willpower abilities observed across individuals and tailor interventions and strategies to meet each person's needs.

4.2 Hormones and Neurotransmitters

Hormones and neurotransmitters are chemical messengers vital in regulating our thoughts, emotions, and behaviors, including our ability to exert willpower. Hormones, produced by glands in the endocrine system, travel through the bloodstream to target cells and tissues, while neurotransmitters are released by neurons in the brain and act on nearby cells. Both messengers contribute to our capacity for self-control, motivation, and perseverance by modulating the activity of the brain structures involved in willpower, such as the prefrontal cortex, anterior cingulate cortex, and striatum.

There was once a community of animals in a lush forest, and they all got along incredibly. Eddie the Elephant, Mandy the Monkey, and Reggie the Rabbit were some animals present. Each animal's hormone and neurotransmitter levels contribute to its strengths and weaknesses.

Eddie the Elephant was known for his incredible memory and ability to focus on tasks for long periods. His brain produced high levels of the neurotransmitter dopamine, which helped him maintain his motivation and concentration. However, Eddie sometimes struggled with impulsivity. His cortisol levels, a stress hormone, could rise quickly in challenging situations, making it difficult for him to stay calm and make thoughtful decisions.

On the other hand, Mandy the Monkey was a social and empathetic creature. Her brain produced high levels of oxytocin, a hormone often referred to as the "love hormone," which contributed to her strong social bonds and ability to understand the emotions of others. However, Mandy's serotonin levels, a neurotransmitter associated with mood regulation, were sometimes low, which made it challenging for her to stay positive and motivated in difficult situations.

Reggie the Rabbit was known for his boundless energy and quick decision-making. His brain produced high levels of norepinephrine, a neurotransmitter involved in arousal and alertness, which kept him vigilant and ready to act. However, Reggie sometimes struggled with anxiety. His adrenaline levels, a hormone involved in the fight-or-flight response, could spike quickly in stressful situations, making it difficult for him to stay calm and think clearly.

A terrible drought struck the forest one day, and the once-lush landscape began to wither and dry up. The animals faced the challenge of finding a new water source to survive. The community formed a team to search for water, and Eddie, Mandy, and Reggie were chosen to lead the mission.

As the trio ventured deep into the forest, they encountered numerous obstacles, such as treacherous terrain, scorching heat, and dwindling food supplies. Despite these challenges, Eddie's ability to concentrate and remember details allowed him to keep track of their path and ensure they got through. Mandy's empathy and social skills helped keep the group's morale high and encouraged cooperation between the team members. Reggie's alertness and quick decision-making enabled him to identify potential dangers and steer the group from harm.

However, each animal also struggled with their weaknesses. Eddie's impulsivity sometimes led him to rush into risky situations without considering the consequences. Mandy's fluctuating mood made it difficult to maintain her motivation when the search for water seemed hopeless. Reggie's anxiety occasionally caused him to become overly cautious, which slowed down their progress.

Throughout their journey, the trio discovered that by acknowledging and understanding the role of their hormones and neurotransmitters, they could better manage their weaknesses and harness their strengths. Eddie learned to pause and take deep breaths when he felt his cortisol levels rising, allowing him to think more clearly and make better decisions. Mandy practiced mindfulness and positive affirmations to boost her serotonin levels, which helped her maintain a positive outlook and stay motivated in the face of adversity. Reggie worked on developing coping strategies, such as deep breathing exercises and visualization techniques, to manage his anxiety and keep his adrenaline levels in check.

As the team continued their search, they eventually stumbled upon a hidden oasis in the forest's heart.

The lush greenery and crystal-clear water perfectly solved their community's water crisis. Eddie, Mandy, and Reggie rejoiced in their success, grateful for their newfound understanding of their unique brain chemistry and its role in their willpower.

Upon returning to their community, the trio shared their experiences and the lessons they had learned about hormones and neurotransmitters. The animals realized that understanding and managing their brain chemistry could improve their self-control, motivation, and perseverance capacity.

The community began to work together to develop strategies to help each animal harness their strengths and overcome their weaknesses. They learned to balance their hormone and neurotransmitter levels through education and practice to face challenges better and achieve their goals.

As time passed, the forest animals became more resilient, resourceful, and united in their efforts to overcome obstacles and thrive in their environment. They understood that their unique brain chemistry was crucial to their willpower. By working together, they could support one another in their journey toward self-improvement and success.

The story of Eddie the Elephant, Mandy the Monkey, and Reggie the Rabbit is a powerful allegory for understanding the role of hormones and neurotransmitters in our capacity for willpower. By acknowledging the impact of these chemical messengers on our thoughts, emotions, and behaviors, we can develop strategies to manage our brain chemistry and cultivate our self-control, motivation, and resilience.

4.3 The Impact of Diet and Exercise

Diet and exercise significantly impact willpower, as they influence the health and function of our brain and body. A well-balanced diet provides essential nutrients that support brain function, such as vitamins, minerals, and healthy fats, which can enhance our cognitive abilities, including self-control, focus, and decision-making.

Conversely, exercise improves blood flow to the brain, reduces inflammation, and stimulates the production of chemicals like endorphins and brain-derived neurotrophic factor (BDNF), boosting mood, motivation, and overall brain health. By prioritizing a healthy diet and regular physical activity, we can support the proper functioning of our brain and body, ultimately enhancing our capacity for willpower.

One real-life athlete whose story exemplifies the impact of diet and exercise on willpower is Michael Phelps, the most decorated Olympian of all time. Phelps' dedication to his training, disciplined diet, and unwavering commitment to his goals provide valuable insights into how prioritizing health and fitness can bolster our willpower and drive us to achieve extraordinary feats.

From a young age, Phelps displayed a natural talent for swimming, but his relentless work ethic and commitment to his training set him apart from other athletes. He spent countless hours in the pool, perfecting his technique, building his endurance, and honing his mental focus. This dedication to his physical fitness allowed him to excel in the sport and cultivated unparalleled willpower and determination.

Phelps' diet played a crucial role in supporting his rigorous training regimen and fueling his extraordinary athletic performance. Consuming up to 12,000 calories per day during his peak training periods, Phelps focused on nutrient-dense foods such as lean proteins, whole grains, fruits, and vegetables. This well-balanced diet provided his body and brain with the necessary fuel to maintain his focus, motivation, and self-discipline, both in and out of the pool.

In addition to his physical training and diet, Phelps also greatly emphasized his mental preparation. He utilized visualization techniques, goal-setting, and positive self-talk to strengthen his mental fortitude and enhance his willpower. By cultivating a strong mindset, Phelps overcame obstacles, persevered through setbacks, and remained steadfast in his pursuit of excellence.

Phelps' unwavering commitment to his goals was evident in his remarkable achievements throughout his career. Throughout five Olympic Games, he amassed 28 medals, 23 of which were gold, setting numerous world records in the process. His incredible accomplishments are partly attributed to his disciplined approach to diet and exercise, which bolstered his willpower and fueled his extraordinary success.

The impact of Phelps' dedication to his health and fitness extended beyond his athletic achievements. His strong willpower and self-discipline also translated into other areas of his life, such as his philanthropic efforts and advocacy for mental health awareness. By leveraging the willpower cultivated through his diet and exercise regimen, Phelps made a significant impact in and out of the pool.

The story of Michael Phelps serves as a powerful reminder of the impact that diet and exercise can have on our willpower and our ability to achieve our goals. By prioritizing our health and well-being, we can cultivate the mental and physical strength necessary to overcome obstacles, persevere through setbacks, and ultimately reach our full potential.

In pursuing our goals, it's essential to remember that our willpower is not a fixed trait but a skill that can be developed and honed over time. By making conscious choices to prioritize our health and well-being, we can nurture our willpower and empower ourselves to achieve extraordinary feats.

The impact of diet and exercise on willpower is an important area of study that continues to evolve as researchers uncover new insights into the complex interplay between our brain, body, and behavior. As we deepen our understanding of these connections, we can develop more effective strategies for cultivating willpower and unlocking our full potential.

By embracing the lessons from Michael Phelps' story and other successful athletes, we can develop a deeper appreciation for the role of diet and exercise in our lives and gain the motivation to make positive changes that support our willpower and overall well-being. Committing to a healthy lifestyle improves our physical health and nurtures our mental strength, enhancing our capacity for self-control, motivation, and perseverance in the face of life's challenges.

Now let's put them together.

Willpower can be envisioned as a grand symphony, with various instruments coming together to create a harmonious and powerful piece of music. The brain structures, hormones, neurotransmitters, diet, and exercise all play crucial roles in this ensemble, each contributing to the melody and rhythm that guide our actions and decisions.

The brain structures serve as the symphony's string section, providing the musical composition's foundation. The prefrontal cortex, amygdala, and other areas of the brain work in concert, regulating our emotions, decision-making, and self-control. Just as the strings set the tone and pace of the music, our brain structures establish the groundwork for our willpower and resilience.

Hormones and neurotransmitters can be compared to the brass and woodwind instruments, adding depth and color to the symphony. Dopamine, serotonin, and cortisol are among the chemicals that influence our mood, energy levels, and motivation. Like the soaring trumpets and emotive clarinets, these hormones and neurotransmitters shape our willpower's dynamic ebb and flow.

Diet and exercise represent the percussion section, providing the rhythm and pulse that drive the symphony forward. A well-balanced diet ensures that our body and mind are fueled with the necessary nutrients to maintain energy and focus, while regular exercise keeps us physically and mentally fit. Like the drums and cymbals that hold the tempo, proper nutrition and exercise help us stay on track and persevere through challenges.

The conductor of this grand symphony symbolizes our conscious choices and actions, guiding the ensemble of our mind and body. With a strong foundation of brain structures, a balanced interplay of hormones and neurotransmitters, and the steady rhythm of diet and exercise, we can confidently lead our symphony toward achieving our goals and overcoming obstacles.

In this magnificent orchestration of life, our willpower serves as the driving force that directs the harmonious collaboration of our mind and body. By nurturing our brain structures, balancing our hormones and neurotransmitters, and prioritizing diet and exercise, we can create a beautiful symphony of willpower, empowering us to reach our full potential and flourish.

Chapter 5: Willpower and Emotions

5.1 The Interplay of Emotions and Willpower

The interplay of emotions and willpower is a complex and fascinating aspect of human psychology. Our emotions can fuel and hinder our ability to exercise willpower, as they influence our motivation, decision-making, and overall mental state. At times, strong emotions can propel us toward our goals, while at other moments, they can undermine our self-control and lead us astray.

Understanding the dynamic relationship between emotions and willpower is crucial in cultivating self-discipline and resilience. Learning to harness our emotions and channel them toward productive endeavors can strengthen our willpower and help us achieve our desired outcomes, even in adversity.

A young man named Thomas Winters once lived in a small, peaceful village. Thomas was known for his exceptional talent as a painter. His works captivated the villagers and visitors alike with their vivid colors, intricate details, and evocative themes. However, Thomas also struggled with intense emotions that often threatened to overwhelm him and diminish his willpower.

As a child, Thomas was highly sensitive to the world around him, and he found solace in the quiet, secluded spaces where he could immerse himself in his art. His paintings provided an outlet for his emotions, allowing him to channel his feelings into something tangible and beautiful. However, as he grew older, Thomas found it increasingly difficult to manage the intensity of his emotions.

One day, a renowned art collector named Elizabeth Hamilton visited the village and was immediately captivated by Thomas's paintings. She offered him the opportunity to study at a prestigious art academy in the city, where he could access renowned mentors and resources. Overwhelmed by the prospect of leaving his quiet village life and facing the unknown, Thomas's emotions began to spiral out of control.

Despite the support and encouragement of his family and friends, Thomas found himself gripped by anxiety, fear, and self-doubt. These feelings threatened to consume him, and he began to retreat further into himself, distancing himself from others and spending more time alone with his thoughts.

Thomas's emotional turmoil gradually began to erode his willpower. He found it difficult to focus on his art, and his once-precise brushstrokes became erratic and unfocused. His paintings, which once inspired awe and admiration, now seemed to lack the magic and emotion that had once defined them.

As the date of his departure from the art academy approached, Thomas's emotions continued to spiral out of control. He began to experience bouts of anger and frustration, lashing out at those around him and alienating those who cared for him most. His relationships with his family and friends deteriorated, leaving him even more isolated and overwhelmed.

Recognizing that he was losing control over his emotions and willpower, Thomas sought help from a wise village elder named Sophia. She listened patiently as Thomas shared his struggles, fears, and dreams.

She advised him to take control of his emotions by practicing mindfulness and learning to observe his thoughts and feelings without judgment or resistance.

Thomas desperately tried to follow Sophia's advice, but the intensity of his emotions grew, and his willpower dwindled. The more he tried to control his feelings, the more they consumed him. His paintings became darker and more chaotic, reflecting his inner turmoil and despair.

As the day of his departure arrived, Thomas was a shadow of his former self, consumed by his emotions and unable to muster the willpower to pursue his dreams. He declined Elizabeth's offer, choosing to remain in the village and continue his emotional struggle.

In the following years, Thomas struggled with his emotions, his willpower slowly eroding. He withdrew further from the world, isolating himself in his small, dimly lit studio, where he painted scenes of sorrow and despair. His once-bright future as a renowned artist seemed to slip further and further out of reach.

Amelia was a single mother, working tirelessly to provide for her young daughter, Lily. Life had dealt Amelia a problematic hand: her husband had passed away in a tragic accident, leaving her to navigate the challenges of parenthood and financial stability independently. Amelia's emotional state was fragile, but she persevered for her daughter's sake.

Despite her struggles, Amelia was passionate about writing. She would pen stories about hope, resilience, and love in her spare time. Her dream was to become a successful author, but the weight of her responsibilities and her emotional turmoil often left her feeling drained and defeated.

One day, as Amelia was walking home from work, she stumbled upon a small community center offering a workshop on emotional management and willpower. Intrigued, she enrolled in the program, hoping to gain insights to help her achieve her goals and provide a better life for Lily.

The workshop was transformative for Amelia. She learned about the power of mindfulness, gratitude, and positive thinking in managing emotions and building willpower. She began to practice these techniques daily, striving to shift her perspective and focus on the positives in her life rather than dwelling on her challenges.

As Amelia's emotional well-being improved, so too did her willpower. She found the energy and motivation to dedicate more time to her writing, staying up late into the night to craft her stories. Her newfound determination caught the attention of a local publisher, who offered her a book deal.

Amelia's book, a collection of uplifting short stories, was an instant hit. Readers resonated with her tales of hope and perseverance, and Amelia quickly gained a devoted fanbase. Her success as an author provided her with the financial stability she had longed for, enabling her to give Lily the life she had always dreamed of.

With her newfound success, Amelia continued to practice the emotional management techniques she had learned in the workshop. She understood that maintaining her willpower required constant effort and dedication, and she committed herself to nurturing her emotional well-being for her own sake and Lily's.

Amelia's story spread far and wide, inspiring others to harness the power of emotional regulation and willpower to overcome adversity. She became a sought-after speaker, sharing her insights and experiences at national conferences, workshops, and seminars.

As Amelia's career flourished, she remained dedicated to her and her daughter's emotional well-being. She understood that life would continue to present challenges and setbacks. Still, she was now equipped with the tools and knowledge to manage her emotions and persevere in adversity.

Amelia's journey is a powerful example of how, even in the most challenging circumstances, one can harness the power of emotional regulation to improve their willpower and ultimately achieve their goals. By learning to manage her emotions, Amelia was able to create a brighter future for herself and her daughter.

5.2 Emotional Regulation and Self-Control

Emotional regulation and self-control are two essential components of willpower. Emotional regulation is managing and responding to one's emotions effectively. At the same time, self-control is the capacity to resist temptation and choose a more productive or beneficial behavior. Emotional regulation and self-control can significantly impact an individual's ability to achieve goals and maintain balance and well-being.

Researchers have recently focused on understanding the cognitive and neurological mechanisms underlying emotional regulation and self-control. It is now widely recognized that these abilities are not fixed traits but skills that can be developed and improved with practice and effort.

One key aspect of emotional regulation involves recognizing and acknowledging one's emotions. By becoming more aware of their emotional states, individuals can better understand the triggers and factors influencing their feelings. This awareness can help them develop more effective strategies for coping with and managing their emotions.

Mindfulness is a powerful tool for promoting emotional regulation. Individuals can develop a greater sense of self-awareness and emotional clarity by learning to be present in the moment and observing one's thoughts and feelings without judgment. This clarity can help them make more informed decisions about responding to their emotions healthily and adaptively.

Cognitive reappraisal is another important aspect of emotional regulation. This strategy involves reframing one's thoughts and perceptions of a situation to change the emotional response. By adopting a more positive or constructive perspective, individuals can reduce the intensity of negative emotions and enhance their ability to cope with challenging situations.

On the other hand, self-control involves the ability to resist impulsive behaviors and make choices that align with one's long-term goals and values. This skill is crucial for maintaining focus, motivation, and discipline in the face of distractions and temptations.

One effective strategy for building self-control is setting clear, attainable goals. By defining specific objectives and breaking them down into manageable steps, individuals can create a roadmap for success to help them stay on track and maintain their focus.

Another important aspect of self-control is learning to delay gratification. This involves resisting the temptation to indulge in immediate rewards or pleasures in favor of pursuing more significant, long-term benefits. Research has shown that individuals who can delay gratification tend to be more successful in various aspects of life, including academics, career, and personal relationships.

Developing a strong sense of self-discipline is also crucial for maintaining self-control. This involves cultivating the ability to persevere and stay committed to one's goals, despite setbacks or challenges. Building self-discipline requires practice, persistence, and patience, but the rewards can be significant in personal growth and achievement.

It is important to recognize that emotional regulation and self-control are interconnected and that improvements in one area can often lead to enhancements in the other. For example, managing one's emotions more effectively can help reduce the intensity of impulsive urges, making it easier to exercise self-control.

Conversely, developing greater self-control can help individuals better manage their emotions by reducing the likelihood of engaging in impulsive, emotion-driven behaviors that may exacerbate negative feelings. Thus, working on both emotional regulation and self-control can synergistically affect overall well-being and success.

Maintaining a healthy lifestyle can also play a crucial role in promoting emotional regulation and self-control. Research has shown that regular exercise, adequate sleep, and a balanced diet can help support cognitive functioning and emotional well-being, making it easier to manage emotions and exercise self-control.

5.3 The Role of Stress and Resilience

Stress and resilience are two factors that can significantly influence willpower. Stress, the body's response to perceived threats or challenges, can deplete an individual's cognitive resources and make it more difficult to exercise self-control. Resilience, conversely, refers to the ability to recover from adversity and bounce back from challenges. High resilience can help individuals maintain their willpower and overcome obstacles, even in the face of significant stress.

The relationship between stress, resilience, and willpower has been a topic of interest for psychologists and researchers for many years. Numerous studies have been conducted to understand how these factors interact and identify strategies for improving resilience and willpower in the face of stress. One notable experiment in this area is the famous marshmallow test, which explores the relationship between self-control, stress, and long-term outcomes.

The marshmallow test, first conducted by psychologist Walter Mischel in the 1960s, involved a group of young children who were given a simple choice: they could either eat one marshmallow immediately or wait for a short period (usually 15 minutes) and receive two marshmallows as a reward for their patience. This experiment was designed to measure the children's ability to delay gratification and exercise self-control in the face of temptation.

Before the test, the children were placed in a room with the marshmallow and told that the researcher would leave for a few minutes. The children were informed that if they could wait until the researcher returned, they would receive the second marshmallow as a reward.

The children were exposed to varying stress levels while waiting alone in the room. Some children found it relatively easy to resist the temptation of the marshmallow, while others struggled to maintain their self-control. The children's reactions to the stress of waiting and resisting temptation were recorded and analyzed.

The researchers found that the children who successfully delayed gratification displayed several common strategies for coping with the stress of the situation. These strategies included distracting themselves by looking away from the marshmallow, covering their eyes, or engaging in self-talk to remind themselves of the goal.

In contrast, the children who were less successful at delaying gratification tended to focus on the marshmallow and its immediate pleasure. This fixation on the temptation made it more difficult for them to exercise self-control and resist the urge to eat the marshmallow.

The marshmallow test has been replicated numerous times, and the results have been remarkably consistent. Children who can delay gratification and exercise self-control in the face of stress tend to have better long-term outcomes, including higher academic achievement, improved social skills, and lower rates of substance abuse and obesity.

These findings suggest that coping with stress and maintaining self-control in challenging situations are critical factors determining an individual's overall success and well-being. Building resilience and developing effective strategies for managing stress can help individuals maintain their willpower and overcome obstacles, even in the face of significant adversity.

In addition to the original marshmallow test, follow-up studies have been conducted to explore the factors contributing to an individual's ability to delay gratification and maintain self-control under stress. These studies have identified several key elements, including the role of parental support, the development of cognitive strategies for managing temptation, and the influence of genetics and temperament.

One follow-up study conducted by Mischel and his colleagues examined the role of parental support in developing self-control and resilience. The researchers found that children who received consistent, nurturing support from their parents were better able to manage stress and maintain self-control in the face of temptation.

Another follow-up study focused on children's cognitive strategies to resist temptation and delay gratification. The researchers found that children who successfully delayed gratification employed various cognitive strategies, such as imagining the marshmallow as a cloud or a picture rather than focusing on its taste and texture. These strategies allowed the children to distance themselves from the immediate temptation and maintain their focus on the long-term goal.

The marshmallow test and its follow-up studies have highlighted the importance of building resilience and developing effective strategies for managing stress to maintain willpower and achieve long-term success. They have also demonstrated that these skills can be cultivated and improved over time through practice and the development of effective coping strategies.

Now let's put them together.

The intricate relationship between emotions, stress, and resilience can be compared to cooking a meal, where willpower acts as the master chef. Just as a chef must skillfully combine and balance various ingredients to create a delicious and satisfying dish, individuals must balance their emotions, manage stress, and cultivate resilience to maintain and strengthen their willpower.

In this culinary metaphor, emotions are the spices and seasonings that give the meal flavor and character. When used skillfully, they can elevate a dish to new heights, making it irresistible and memorable. However, when emotions are not managed properly, they can overpower the dish, making it unpalatable and difficult to enjoy. Likewise, individuals must learn to regulate their emotions to prevent them from overwhelming their willpower and hindering their progress.

Stress can be likened to the stove or oven heat, which is essential for transforming raw ingredients into a delicious meal. At the right level, stress can help individuals stay focused and motivated, enabling them to reach their goals. However, when the heat becomes too high or uneven, it can scorch the meal, making it difficult to salvage. Similarly, individuals must learn to manage stress to prevent it from consuming their willpower and derailing their efforts.

Resilience, on the other hand, can be compared to the quality and freshness of the ingredients. High-quality ingredients can withstand the heat and the seasoning, resulting in a delicious and satisfying meal. As chefs must select and prepare the best ingredients, individuals must cultivate resilience to navigate life's challenges and persevere in adversity.

When emotions, stress, and resilience are skillfully balanced and combined, the result is a delectable and nourishing meal that reflects the individual's unique tastes and preferences. By mastering this culinary art, individuals can harness their willpower to create a life filled with satisfaction, achievement, and well-being.

Chapter 6: Social and Environmental Influences on Willpower

6.1 The Power of Social Support

Social support plays a crucial role in influencing an individual's willpower. Having a network of friends, family, and colleagues who provide encouragement, guidance, and assistance can significantly impact a person's ability to persevere and overcome challenges. Social support can act as a buffer against stress, reducing the negative impact of adversity on willpower and helping individuals stay on track toward their goals.

The power of social support can manifest in various ways, such as providing emotional encouragement, sharing advice, or offering practical assistance. In addition to reducing stress, social support can enhance an individual's motivation, self-esteem, and self-efficacy, critical willpower components. Social support can empower individuals to overcome obstacles and reach their full potential by fostering a sense of belonging and connection.

A remarkable example of the power of social support can be seen in the true story of Aron Ralston, an American outdoorsman whose incredible tale of survival captured the world's attention. In 2003, Ralston embarked on a solo hiking trip in the remote canyons of southeastern Utah. While navigating a narrow slot canyon, Ralston became trapped when an 800-pound boulder dislodged and pinned his right arm against the canyon wall.

For five days, Ralston remained trapped, surviving on a small ration of water and food while attempting various methods to free himself. As his situation became increasingly dire, Ralston began to lose hope and realized he might not survive. However, thoughts of his family and friends, and the realization that they would be devastated by his death, provided him with the emotional support he needed to continue fighting.

Faced with the prospect of dying in the canyon, Ralston made the agonizing decision to amputate his arm with a dull multi-tool to free himself from the boulder. Despite the excruciating pain and the immense physical and mental challenges, Ralston completed the amputation, applied a makeshift tourniquet, and rappelled down a 65-foot cliff to seek help.

Ralston's incredible story of survival underscores the power of social support in maintaining willpower, even under the most extreme circumstances. The emotional connection to his loved ones was a vital source of strength, motivating Ralston to persevere and ultimately save his life.

Following his ordeal, Ralston's story gained widespread media attention. He became a motivational speaker, sharing his experience and the lessons he learned about the importance of social support and willpower. Ralston's story was later adapted into the 2010 film "127 Hours," starring James Franco, further highlighting social support's crucial role in overcoming adversity.

The impact of Ralston's story extends far beyond his own experience, inspiring countless others to face their challenges and recognize the power of social support. His tale is a testament to the resilience of the human spirit and the incredible strength that can be drawn from the connections we share with others.

In 2010, the tragic story of Joyce Carol Vincent, a British woman whose death went unnoticed for more than two years, captured the media's attention and served as a stark reminder of the importance of social support.

Joyce Vincent was a vibrant and seemingly well-liked woman in her late thirties. She had previously worked in the financial industry and had many interests, including music and film. However, despite her appearance of success, she struggled with personal issues, such as a history of abusive relationships and a lack of stable employment. Eventually, her life went downward, and she became increasingly isolated from friends and family.

In December 2003, Vincent's body was discovered in her London flat by housing officials who had come to repossess the property due to unpaid rent. Shockingly, she had been dead for more than two years; her body lay undisturbed in her apartment all that time. The cause of death could not be determined due to the advanced state of decomposition, but no foul play was suspected.

The fact that Vincent's death went unnoticed for so long raises troubling questions about the role of social support in her life. Despite having once been a sociable and outgoing person, she appeared to have become increasingly disconnected from her social network in the years leading up to her death.

The lack of social support may have contributed to Vincent's inability to overcome the challenges she faced in her life, such as her struggles with abusive relationships, unstable employment, and mental health issues. Without a strong network of friends and family to provide encouragement, advice, and assistance, her willpower may have been eroded, making it more difficult for her to break free from the downward spiral she found herself in.

Vincent's tragic story is a cautionary tale about the importance of social support in maintaining willpower and overcoming adversity. Her death highlights the need for society to be more vigilant in looking out for individuals struggling in isolation and ensure they have access to the resources and support they need to thrive.

In the wake of Vincent's story, various initiatives have been launched to raise awareness of the issue of social isolation and to provide resources for individuals who may be at risk. These efforts serve as a reminder of the crucial role that social support plays in maintaining willpower and improving the overall well-being of individuals.

In today's increasingly interconnected world, social support is more accessible than ever. Through digital platforms and online communities, individuals can find encouragement, advice, and camaraderie from like-minded individuals, regardless of geographical distance. This virtual social support can be valuable for maintaining willpower and overcoming challenges.

6.2 The Impact of Culture and Society

Culture and society have a significant impact on an individual's willpower. The values, beliefs, and norms ingrained in a particular culture can either facilitate or hinder the development and expression of willpower. Societal expectations, such as success, work ethic, and self-discipline, can shape individuals' motivation and determination to achieve their goals. Additionally, cultural factors like individualism or collectivism can influence how people approach challenges, manage stress, and develop resilience.

Moreover, societal influences, such as education, economic conditions, and social policies, can create an environment that either fosters or impedes the cultivation of willpower. Access to resources, social support, and opportunities can be crucial in shaping an individual's ability to persevere and overcome obstacles. By understanding the impact of culture and society on willpower, we can better recognize the complex interplay of factors contributing to individual success and resilience.

One powerful example of the impact of culture and society on willpower can be seen in the story of Malala Yousafzai, a Pakistani activist for female education and the youngest Nobel Prize laureate. Born in Swat Valley, Pakistan, Malala grew up in a society where the Taliban, an extremist group, enforced strict rules and regulations, particularly on women's rights and education. Despite the oppressive environment, Malala's father, Ziauddin Yousafzai, an educator and activist, encouraged her to pursue education and speak out against the Taliban's oppressive regime.

Malala began blogging for BBC Urdu under a pseudonym as a young girl, sharing her experiences and advocating for girls' education. However, her activism attracted the attention of the Taliban, and in October 2012, Malala was shot in the head by a Taliban gunman while on her way home from school. Miraculously, she survived the attack and was flown to the United Kingdom for treatment and rehabilitation.

Malala's story highlights the incredible willpower that can be forged in the face of cultural and societal adversity. Despite growing up in a society that sought to silence and oppress her, Malala was determined to fight for her right to education and the rights of other girls in Pakistan. Her strong willpower can be attributed to the support and encouragement she received from her family and her deep-rooted belief in the power of education to transform lives and break the cycle of oppression.

Since her recovery, Malala has continued her activism on a global scale, establishing the Malala Fund to promote education for girls worldwide and becoming the youngest-ever recipient of the Nobel Peace Prize in 2014. Her story is a powerful reminder of culture and society's impact on an individual's willpower and the importance of fighting for one's beliefs, even in the face of seemingly insurmountable obstacles.

Another real-life story that illustrates the impact of culture and society on willpower is that of the Lost Boys of Sudan. The Lost Boys were a group of over 20,000 young boys who were displaced and orphaned during the Second Sudanese Civil War (1983-2005).

The war destroyed villages, families were torn apart, and an entire generation of children was forced to fend for themselves.

The Lost Boys, some as young as six, began a treacherous journey from Sudan to Ethiopia, seeking refuge from the conflict. They walked for months, covering over a thousand miles on foot, facing starvation, dehydration, and attacks from wild animals and enemy soldiers. Many did not survive the journey. Those who made it to Ethiopia were forced to flee again when the situation became unstable, eventually finding refuge in Kenya at the Kakuma refugee camp.

The story of the Lost Boys showcases the incredible willpower of these young boys who faced unimaginable hardships yet persevered to survive. Their resilience can be attributed to their strong sense of community and the group's shared experience. They relied on each other for support, motivation, and protection, demonstrating the power of social connections in fostering willpower.

In 2001, the United States began a resettlement program for the Lost Boys, allowing them to build new lives in America. Upon arriving in the U.S., they faced new challenges, such as adapting to a new culture, learning English, and finding employment. Despite these obstacles, many of the Lost Boys have shown remarkable determination and willpower to succeed in their new lives.

One of the Lost Boys, John Dau, has been particularly successful, becoming a prominent human rights activist and the founder of the John Dau Foundation, an organization focused on providing healthcare and education to communities in South Sudan. Dau's story highlights the role of culture and society in shaping an individual's willpower and the importance of resilience and determination in overcoming adversity.

6.3 The Effect of Environment and Surroundings

The environment and surroundings we live, work, and socialize in can significantly impact our willpower. Our surroundings can support or hinder our ability to focus, make decisions, and exert self-control. Factors such as noise levels, lighting, cleanliness, and the availability of resources can all influence our mental state and overall well-being. Furthermore, social environments, such as our relationships with friends, family, and colleagues, can also affect our motivation, resilience, and determination to achieve our goals.

The design of our physical spaces and the quality of our social environments can play a crucial role in shaping our willpower. By creating spaces that promote relaxation, focus, and positive social interactions, we can better support individuals in cultivating willpower and overcoming challenges. Recognizing the impact of our environment and surroundings on willpower is an essential step toward fostering resilience and personal success.

The story of J.K. Rowling, the renowned author of the Harry Potter series, provides a powerful example of how the environment and surroundings can impact an individual's willpower. Before her rise to fame, Rowling was a struggling single mother, living on welfare in a small flat in Edinburgh, Scotland. At the time, her living conditions could have been better, with little writing space and limited resources to support her creative pursuits.

Despite these challenges, Rowling found solace and inspiration in Edinburgh. The city's historic streets, winding alleys, and impressive architecture were the backdrop for the magical world she would create in her Harry Potter novels. To escape the distractions of her small flat, Rowling would often write in local cafes, such as The Elephant House, where she found the peace and focus she needed to bring her stories to life.

Despite her challenging circumstances, Rowling's perseverance and determination to succeed were partly fueled by the supportive and inspiring environment she found in Edinburgh. The city's rich history and vibrant culture provided a nurturing environment that helped Rowling cultivate her willpower and ultimately achieve her goal of becoming a successful author.

Shawn Achor is a positive psychology expert and the author of "*The Happiness Advantage*" and "Big Potential". In one of the interviews, Achor discussed the impact of our environment and surroundings on happiness, well-being, and willpower.

Interviewer: Shawn, thank you for joining us today. Please explain how our environment and surroundings can impact our happiness and willpower.

Shawn Achor: Absolutely. Our environment plays a crucial role in shaping our mindset, emotions, and motivation. A well-designed environment can help reduce stress, increase focus, and promote positive behaviors. On the other hand, a chaotic or negative environment can make it difficult for us to maintain our willpower and achieve our goals.

Interviewer: Can you explain how people can optimize their environment to improve their willpower and well-being?

Shawn Achor: Certainly. One example is decluttering and organizing your workspace. A cluttered environment can create mental clutter, making it difficult to focus and stay productive.

Keeping our workspace organized can improve our mental clarity and increase our ability to stay on task.

Another example is to surround yourself with positive social connections. Our relationships can either support or drain our willpower. We can increase our motivation, resilience, and overall well-being by fostering positive relationships and spending time with people who encourage and uplift us.

Interviewer: How can organizations create a more supportive environment for their employees to enhance willpower and happiness in the workplace?

Shawn Achor: Organizations can promote a positive environment by creating spaces conducive to focus, relaxation, and collaboration. This can include providing access to natural light, creating quiet areas for focused work, and designing communal spaces that encourage positive employee interactions.

Additionally, organizations should recognize the importance of fostering a supportive and inclusive culture that values employees' well-being and encourages them to maintain a healthy work-life balance.

Interviewer: Thank you, Shawn. Your insights on the importance of our environment and surroundings in shaping our willpower and happiness are precious.

Shawn Achor: You're welcome. I'm glad I could share my thoughts on this important topic. By being aware of the impact of our environment and taking steps to create supportive surroundings, we can significantly improve our ability to stay motivated, focused, and resilient in the face of challenges.

One social study theory that illustrates the effect of environment and surroundings on willpower is the "Broken Windows Theory." This theory was first introduced by social scientists James Q. Wilson and George L. Kelling in 1982. The Broken Windows Theory posits that visible signs of disorder and neglect in a community, such as broken windows, graffiti, and litter, can lead to increased crime and antisocial behavior. This is because a disordered environment signals that the area needs to be better cared for and that the community norms are not enforced.

The Broken Windows Theory can be extended to understand the impact of environment and surroundings on willpower. When an individual is surrounded by a disorganized, chaotic, or neglected environment, it can create a sense of disorder and a lack of control. This can, in turn, make it more difficult for a person to exert self-discipline and maintain their willpower.

On the other hand, when an individual is in a clean, well-organized, and aesthetically pleasing environment, they may feel a greater sense of control and calm. This can help them to focus better, make more thoughtful decisions, and maintain their willpower to achieve their goals.

Various empirical studies have supported the Broken Windows Theory, which has found a correlation between environmental factors and an individual's behavior. For example, a study by researchers at the University of Groningen in the Netherlands found that participants in a clean, orderly room were likelier to make healthier food choices and donate more money to charity than those in a messy, messy, messy, cluttered room. This study suggests that our environment and surroundings significantly impact our decision-making ability and willpower.

Now let's put them together again.

Willpower can be compared to a ship navigating through the vast ocean. A ship's success in reaching its destination relies on various factors, much like how willpower depends on the interplay of social support, culture and society, and the environment and surroundings.

The crew members aboard the ship represent the social support that influences our willpower. Just like how a skilled and supportive crew can navigate the ship through rough waters, the encouragement and help we receive from friends, family, and mentors can bolster our willpower when faced with challenges. In contrast, a dysfunctional or unsupportive crew may lead the ship astray, much like the absence of social support can weaken our resolve.

Our culture and society can be likened to the ocean currents and trade winds that propel the ship forward. When societal norms and values align with our goals, we are carried along with the flow, which makes it easier to maintain our willpower. However, when these currents and winds are against us, it requires extra effort and determination to forge our path and achieve our goals.

Lastly, the ship's environment and surroundings—its overall cleanliness, organization, and resources—mirror the role of our physical environment in shaping our willpower. A well-maintained and well-equipped ship allows the crew to perform at their best, helping the ship sail smoothly through the ocean. Similarly, a conducive environment that is clean, organized, and filled with positive stimuli can enhance our focus, motivation, and resilience.

When all these factors unite in harmony—the crew working as a team, the currents and winds favorable, and the ship's environment optimized—the ship sails effortlessly toward its destination. Likewise, when we receive strong social support, navigate within a supportive culture and society, and cultivate a positive environment, our willpower can be fortified, enabling us to accomplish our goals and overcome the challenges that come our way.

Chapter 7: Willpower and Habits

7.1 Forming and Breaking Habits

In willpower, forming and breaking habits is crucial in determining our ability to achieve our goals and lead successful lives. Whether beneficial or detrimental, habits can significantly impact our daily routines, decision-making, and overall quality of life. Understanding how to form positive and break harmful habits can effectively harness our willpower and create lasting change.

Phillippa Lally and her colleagues at University College London conducted a groundbreaking study on habit formation. In this study, Lally investigated how long it takes to form a new habit and what factors contribute to habit formation. Participants were asked to choose a healthy habit they wanted to develop, such as exercising, eating fruit, or drinking water, and were instructed to perform the habit daily for 12 weeks. They also self-reported their habit strength and adherence throughout the study.

The study involved 96 participants, ranging from 18 to 63 years old, recruited from the general population through advertisements in local newspapers and online.

The participants were asked to choose a simple, health-related behavior they wanted to turn into a habit. The selected behavior had to be something they did not currently do and could be performed daily, such as exercising, eating fruit, or drinking a glass of water. The participants were instructed to perform the chosen behavior daily in the same context (e.g., after breakfast) for 12 weeks. They were provided with a logbook to record their daily performance of the behavior, as well as any missed instances.

In addition to tracking their daily performance, participants were asked to complete a self-report habit index (SRHI) questionnaire daily. The SRHI is a tool designed to measure the strength of a habit by asking participants to rate various statements related to the behavior on a scale of 1 (strongly disagree) to 7 (strongly agree). Statements included items such as "I do this automatically," "I do this without thinking," and "I would find it hard not to do this." Participants completed the SRHI daily, providing a measure of how automatic the behavior felt to them over time.

Throughout the 12 weeks, participants submitted their logbooks and SRHI scores to the research team via email or regular mail. The researchers then analyzed the data to determine the average number of days it took for the new behavior to reach its peak habit strength or the point at which it became an automatic part of the participants' daily routines.

The results of Lally's study showed that, on average, it took 66 days for a new habit to become automatic. However, the time it took varied widely among participants, ranging from 18 to 254 days. The study also found that the complexity of the behavior, individual differences in motivation and self-discipline, and prior experience with the behavior influenced the time it took to form a habit.

Lally's study provides valuable insights into the process of habit formation, emphasizing that persistence and consistency are key factors in developing new habits. It also highlights the importance of understanding individual differences and the role of context in habit formation, which can help people effectively harness their willpower to make lasting changes in their lives.

One critical aspect of using willpower to form good habits is setting realistic and achievable goals. Individuals can maintain motivation and avoid becoming overwhelmed by breaking down a larger goal into smaller, manageable tasks. This incremental approach enables individuals to experience a series of successes, bolstering their willpower and increasing the likelihood of forming a new habit.

Consistency is another essential factor in effectively using willpower for habit formation. Individuals can create a cue that triggers the desired behavior by dedicating a specific time and context to a new habit. Over time, this consistent cue-action pairing helps to strengthen the habit and make it more automatic, reducing the need for conscious willpower to maintain the behavior.

Monitoring progress is also crucial for using willpower effectively in forming good habits. Regularly assessing one's performance through self-reflection or tracking tools can help individuals identify areas for improvement and adjust their strategies accordingly. This self-awareness promotes more efficient use of willpower, as individuals can target their efforts toward specific challenges.

Developing strategies to cope with setbacks is another important aspect of using willpower for habit formation. As individuals encounter obstacles or temporary lapses in their new habits, it is essential to maintain a growth mindset and view these instances as learning opportunities. By reframing setbacks as chances to refine their approach, individuals can prevent discouragement and sustain their willpower to continue working toward their goals.

In addition to personal strategies, social support can significantly enhance the effective use of willpower in forming good habits. By seeking encouragement and accountability from friends, family, or peers, individuals can reinforce their commitment to change and gain valuable insights from others who share similar goals.

This social support can help bolster willpower, making it easier to stay on track and achieve habit formation.

Mindfulness is another valuable tool for using willpower effectively in habit formation. Individuals can recognize and better manage internal triggers that may hinder their progress by cultivating awareness of one's thoughts, feelings, and bodily sensations. Mindfulness practices, such as meditation, can strengthen self-control and enable individuals to direct their willpower toward their habit-formation goals effectively.

Leveraging the power of positive reinforcement can also aid in skillfully using willpower for habit formation. By rewarding themselves for small successes, individuals can create a positive feedback loop that increases motivation and strengthens their resolve. These rewards can be tangible, like a treat or a particular purchase, or intangible, such as a moment of relaxation or a mental pat on the back.

It is essential to recognize that willpower is finite, and individuals must prioritize their habit-formation goals to maximize their effectiveness. By focusing on one or two key habits at a time, individuals can conserve their willpower and increase their chances of success. Once a habit becomes more ingrained and requires less conscious effort, individuals can shift their focus to additional habit formation goals.

In conclusion, skillfully using willpower to form good habits involves:

- Setting realistic goals.
- Maintaining consistency.
- Monitoring progress.
- Coping with setbacks.
- Seeking social support.
- Practicing mindfulness.
- Leveraging positive reinforcement.
- Prioritizing habit-formation efforts.

By applying these strategies, individuals can effectively harness their willpower to create lasting and beneficial life changes.

7.2 Habit Loop

The Habit Loop, described by Charles Duhigg in his book "The Power of Habit," plays a crucial role in understanding the relationship between habits and willpower. The loop consists of three main components: the cue, the routine, and the reward. By examining these elements and their interplay, we can better comprehend how willpower influences habit formation and maintenance.

The impact of willpower on the Habit Loop becomes apparent when we try to change or establish new habits. It takes significant mental effort and self-control to override the automaticity of ingrained routines. In this process, the role of willpower is to help us resist the urge to follow our old patterns and instead choose a more desired behavior.

When attempting to modify a habit, one strategy involves altering the cues that trigger the routine. We can gradually reshape our habits by being mindful of the cues and using willpower to change our responses. For example, if someone struggles with procrastination and the cue is sitting down at their computer, they might choose to use their willpower to avoid distractions like social media or email and instead focus on their work.

Another approach to leveraging willpower in the Habit Loop is changing the routine. This could involve replacing a less desirable behavior with a more positive one using the same cue and reward. For instance, if the habit is snacking on junk food when feeling stressed, the individual could consciously choose to go for a walk or meditate instead, providing a healthier outlet for stress relief.

Furthermore, willpower can be applied to create more compelling rewards for desired habits. Since rewards are essential for reinforcing new routines, it's crucial to ensure that they are meaningful and satisfying. By using willpower to identify and implement effective rewards, we can make the new habits more appealing and easier to maintain.

It's essential to recognize that willpower is a finite resource, and relying solely on it to change habits can be exhausting and unsustainable. However, once new routines are established and automatic, the demand for willpower decreases, making it easier to maintain the new habits over time.

In 2010, a story emerged about Sarah Hornibrook, who used her willpower to change her habit loop, resulting in a remarkable transformation. Sarah, a mother of two from the United Kingdom, weighed 308 pounds and struggled with obesity for most of her life. Her unhealthy habits were deeply ingrained, leading to various health issues, including sleep apnea and high blood pressure.

Sarah's cue was stress, which led to overeating and consuming high-calorie, unhealthy foods to cope. The reward she received was a temporary relief from stress, which reinforced the habit. This loop perpetuated her weight gain and worsened her health over the years.

One day, Sarah saw a photograph of herself at a family event and was devastated by the image. This was a turning point for her, and she realized that she needed to make significant changes in her life to regain control of her health and well-being. Sarah used her willpower to break the destructive habit loop and create new, healthier habits.

Sarah identified her stress cue and decided to replace her unhealthy eating routine with healthier alternatives. She began incorporating regular exercise into her daily routine, starting with short walks and gradually increasing her physical activity. In addition to exercise, Sarah used her willpower to change her diet, replacing high-calorie, processed foods with nutritious whole foods like fruits, vegetables, and lean proteins.

The reward for her new habits was improved health and well-being, reinforcing her commitment to change. As Sarah began to experience the positive effects of her new habits, her willpower was strengthened, making it easier to maintain her new routines.

Over time, Sarah lost an astounding 168 pounds and transformed her life. Her sleep apnea disappeared, her blood pressure normalized, and her energy levels soared. She became a role model for her children and inspired others struggling with weight and health.

Sarah's story was covered by various news outlets and media platforms, highlighting her incredible journey and the power of willpower in breaking the habit loop. Her success demonstrated that overcoming even the most ingrained habits with determination, hard work, and a strategic approach to habit change is possible.

Today, Sarah maintains her healthy lifestyle, proving that sustainable habit change is achievable. Her story is a testament to the power of willpower and the potential for transformation when committed to making a change.

In conclusion, the Habit Loop is a powerful framework that reveals the complex relationship between habits and willpower. By understanding the loop's components and utilizing willpower strategically, we can effectively change our habits to improve our lives and achieve our goals.

7.3 Building Keystone Habits

Building keystone habits is crucial to harnessing willpower to create lasting change. Keystone habits are foundational behaviors that, when cultivated, ripple effect on other areas of a person's life. They create a domino effect, leading to positive habits and improvements in various aspects of life.

The power of keystone habits lies in their ability to create a sense of structure and stability, providing a framework for other habits to be built upon. One typical example of a keystone habit is regular exercise. When people commit to exercising consistently, they often find that other positive habits, such as eating more healthily, sleeping better, and managing stress more effectively, naturally follow suit.

To build keystone habits, it is essential to identify the habits that can act as a foundation for other positive changes. This may involve reflecting on personal values, goals, and the areas of life that require improvement. Once a keystone habit has been identified, developing a plan for incorporating it into daily life is crucial.

An effective way to start building a keystone habit is to set specific, measurable, achievable, relevant, and time-bound (SMART) goals. This approach helps to provide clarity and direction, increasing the likelihood of success. For example, if the keystone habit is regular exercise, a SMART goal might be to commit to walking for 30 minutes five times a week for the next month.

Next, it is essential to establish cues and rewards that reinforce the keystone habit. As with any habit, identifying the cues that trigger the habit, developing a consistent routine, and focusing on the rewards associated with the habit can help to solidify the behavior. In the case of regular exercise, the cue could be setting out workout clothes the night before, the routine would be the workout itself, and the reward might be the feeling of accomplishment after completing the exercise.

One of the keys to building keystone habits is consistency. It is important to commit to the habit, even when motivation wanes or obstacles arise. Over time, as the habit becomes ingrained, the willpower required to maintain the behavior decreases, and the habit becomes an automatic part of daily life.

Building keystone habits strengthens willpower and leads to a sense of self-efficacy and empowerment. As individuals experience the positive effects of their keystone habits, they gain confidence to create lasting change in other areas of their lives. This, in turn, fuels further personal growth and the development of other positive habits.

David Goggins is a retired Navy SEAL, ultra-endurance athlete, and motivational speaker. His transformation from an overweight, depressed young man to an extraordinary athlete has been widely covered by the media. It serves as a testament to the power of willpower and keystone habits.

David Goggins was once 300 pounds and worked as a pest control exterminator. Unhappy with his life and depression, he made a drastic change. Watching a documentary on Navy SEALs inspired him to pursue a career in the military. However, he lost over 100 pounds in just three months to qualify for the training program. This was the turning point, where he used his willpower to transform himself completely.

Goggins committed to a rigorous exercise routine, which became his keystone habit. He started running and cycling daily, pushing through the pain and discomfort accompanying his initial attempts. As he built up his exercise habit, he also began to change his diet, cutting out junk food and focusing on nutritious meals. The discipline he developed from exercising consistently started to spill over into other areas of his life.

His dedication and willpower paid off. Goggins lost weight, qualified for Navy SEAL training, and became one of the most accomplished endurance athletes in the world. He has completed multiple ultra-marathons and triathlons and even set the world record for the most pull-ups in 24 hours.

As Goggins continued to develop his keystone habit of regular exercise, he found that it improved his physical health and helped him build mental resilience. In multiple interviews and his bestselling book, "Can't Hurt Me," Goggins emphasizes the importance of mental toughness and pushing through personal limitations.

The story of David Goggins demonstrates the power of willpower and keystone habits in transforming one's life. By focusing on a single foundational habit – in Goggins' case, exercise – he created a ripple effect of positive change that ultimately led him to overcome his past, achieve extraordinary accomplishments, and inspire countless others.

Now let's put them together again.

The journey of harnessing willpower to form and break habits, understand the habit loop, and build keystone habits can be compared to constructing a solid, well-designed building. Like an architect, one must consider the blueprint, the foundation, and the materials to create a structure that stands the test of time.

In this metaphor, forming and breaking habits represent the blueprint, the initial plan that guides the overall construction. To build a strong, durable structure, it's crucial to eliminate any weak points and incorporate elements that ensure stability. Similarly, to create a life of success and fulfillment, one must identify and break harmful habits while intentionally forming positive ones that support personal growth.

The habit loop symbolizes the foundation of the building. Just as a solid foundation is critical for a building's stability, understanding the habit loop – the cue, routine, and reward – is essential for maintaining and reinforcing positive habits. One can modify or replace the routine by being mindful of the triggers and rewards associated with a habit, effectively altering the habit loop and building a stronger foundation for personal growth.

Finally, keystone habits represent the high-quality materials used in construction. These habits have a transformative impact on multiple aspects of life, just as using robust and reliable materials ensures the building's longevity and resilience. One can create a domino effect that improves various areas of life by cultivating keystone habits, such as regular exercise, healthy eating, or consistent sleep.

In summary, harnessing willpower to change habits is like constructing a solid, well-designed building. By developing a blueprint of positive habits, laying a strong foundation through understanding the habit loop, and using keystone habits as high-quality building materials, one can create a life that stands tall and withstands the tests of time and adversity.

Chapter 8: Strategies for Enhancing Willpower

8.1 Mindfulness and Meditation

Mindfulness and meditation have long been recognized as powerful tools for enhancing willpower. Rooted in ancient traditions, these practices have gained significant attention in recent years due to their scientifically proven benefits. Both mindfulness and meditation involve:

- Directing one's attention and focus to the present moment.
- Cultivating non-judgmental awareness of thoughts.
- Emotions.
- Physical sensations.

Mindfulness is a mental state where one is fully present, engaged in the current activity, and calmly acknowledging and accepting one's feelings, thoughts, and bodily sensations. Incorporating mindfulness into everyday life can improve focus, reduce stress, and increase self-awareness, allowing individuals to make more conscious decisions and exercise greater self-control.

Meditation is training the mind to achieve heightened consciousness and awareness. Various forms of meditation exist, including concentration meditation, which focuses on a single point, and mindfulness meditation, which emphasizes open monitoring of one's thoughts and emotions. Regular meditation has been shown to boost willpower by strengthening the prefrontal cortex, the brain region responsible for executive functions like decision-making, self-control, and attention.

Research has demonstrated that mindfulness and meditation can increase gray matter in the prefrontal cortex and improve connectivity between different brain regions, resulting in better impulse control and decision-making capabilities. These practices can also reduce stress levels, known to deplete willpower, by decreasing the production of the stress hormone cortisol.

One notable study found that participants who underwent an eight-week mindfulness-based stress reduction program experienced significant improvements in self-control, attention, and emotional regulation. These individuals also exhibited reduced stress levels and increased activation in the prefrontal cortex when faced with challenging situations.

Incorporating mindfulness and meditation into daily routines can be relatively simple. Beginners can start with a few minutes of focused breathing or guided meditation sessions daily. As one becomes more comfortable with the practice, the duration and variety of meditation techniques can be expanded to support the development of willpower further.

Practicing mindfulness and meditation consistently can help individuals recognize their triggers, better understand their habitual responses, and develop healthier coping mechanisms. By fostering self-awareness, these practices empower people to make conscious choices and exert greater control over their actions, ultimately strengthening their willpower and setting them on the path to personal growth and success.

Dan Harris, an ABC News anchor, is a powerful example of how mindfulness and meditation can enhance willpower. Harris worked as a television journalist for several years, covering high-stress stories such as wars and natural disasters. In 2004, while reporting live on Good Morning America, Harris experienced a panic attack on air. This event served as a wake-up call for him to reevaluate his mental health and coping mechanisms.

Harris began researching various ways to manage stress and anxiety, eventually stumbling upon the practice of mindfulness meditation. Skeptical at first, he decided to give it a try, following an evidence-based approach rooted in scientific research.

To learn more about mindfulness meditation, Harris started attending workshops, reading books, and consulting experts in the field. One of the key resources he discovered was the work of Dr. Jon Kabat-Zinn, a renowned mindfulness researcher and founder of the Mindfulness-Based Stress Reduction (MBSR) program.

Harris then embarked on a daily meditation practice, starting with just a few minutes of focused breathing each day. Gradually, he increased the duration and incorporated various mindfulness techniques such as body scans and loving-kindness meditation.

As he deepened his practice, Harris noticed significant improvements in his ability to manage stress and anxiety. Meditation helped him become more aware of his thoughts and emotions, enabling him to recognize his triggers and respond more skillfully to challenging situations.

Harris employed an anchor, such as the breath or a mantra, to ground himself in the present moment. Whenever he noticed his mind wandering, he would gently return his focus to the anchor, helping him cultivate greater concentration and self-awareness.

To further enhance his meditation practice, Harris attended meditation retreats, where he spent several days in silence, focusing on his breath and observing his thoughts. These retreats allowed him to delve deeper into mindfulness and experience the transformative power of sustained practice.

Another critical aspect of Harris's journey was his commitment to consistency. He made meditation a non-negotiable part of his daily routine, ensuring that he maintained his practice even when traveling or facing a busy schedule.

Harris's transformation was so profound that he wrote a bestselling book, "10% Happier," detailing his journey into mindfulness and meditation. He also launched a podcast and a meditation app, both under the same name, to help others discover the benefits of these practices.

From a biological standpoint, mindfulness meditation and its impact on enhancing willpower can be traced to brain structure and function changes. Research has shown that regular meditation can alter several brain areas, particularly those associated with self-regulation, emotional control, and stress response.

One key area is the prefrontal cortex, which plays a crucial role in executive functions such as decision-making, goal-setting, and impulse control. Studies have demonstrated that meditation can increase the thickness and activity in this region, leading to enhanced willpower and self-control. By strengthening the prefrontal cortex, individuals like Dan Harris become better equipped to manage stress, resist impulses, and maintain focus on their goals.

Another vital brain region influenced by meditation is the amygdala, which is responsible for processing emotions and generating the body's stress response. Research has found that mindfulness meditation can decrease the size of the amygdala and reduce its reactivity to stressors. This change in the brain's emotional center can help individuals like Harris become less susceptible to anxiety and emotional overwhelm, allowing them to maintain greater emotional stability and willpower.

Mindfulness meditation also impacts the anterior cingulate cortex (ACC), which is involved in attention regulation and error detection. An active ACC can help individuals recognize when their thoughts or actions are straying from their goals, enabling them to correct course more effectively. Meditation has increased connectivity between the ACC and other brain regions, promoting better attention control and enhancing willpower.

In addition to these structural changes, meditation has been shown to influence the levels of neurotransmitters and hormones in the brain, such as dopamine, serotonin, and cortisol. These neurochemicals play a role in modulating mood, motivation, and stress response. By practicing mindfulness meditation, individuals can promote a healthier balance of these chemicals, thereby supporting a more resilient and adaptive mindset.

To sum up, the biological changes brought about by mindfulness meditation, as demonstrated by Dan Harris's story, can be linked to enhanced willpower through alterations in brain structure, function, and neurochemistry. These changes contribute to improved self-regulation, emotional control, and stress management, which are crucial for maintaining strong willpower and achieving one's goals.

8.2 Goal Setting and Implementation Intentions

Goal setting and implementation intentions are powerful strategies for enhancing willpower and achieving success in various aspects of life. These techniques help individuals channel their energy and focus toward specific objectives, making staying committed and maintaining self-discipline easier.

Goal setting involves defining clear, realistic, measurable objectives aligned with one's values and priorities. By setting well-defined goals, individuals provide a roadmap for success and create a sense of purpose that can help maintain motivation and commitment. The SMART (Specific, Measurable, Achievable, Relevant, and Time-bound) criteria are widely used for setting practical goals. It ensures that objectives are clear, manageable, and aligned with one's vision.

On the other hand, implementation intentions involve creating concrete action plans that specify how, when, and where an individual will work toward their goals. This strategy helps bridge the gap between intention and action, making individuals more likely to follow through on their commitments. For example, instead of merely stating the desire to exercise more, one might create an implementation intention such as "I will go for a 30-minute walk every weekday at 6:00 PM in the park near my house." This level of specificity makes it easier to integrate new habits into daily routines and increases the likelihood of success.

A key aspect of implementation intentions is using "if-then" plans, which involve identifying potential obstacles and devising strategies to overcome them in advance. By anticipating challenges and proactively planning for them, individuals can minimize the impact of setbacks and maintain their willpower in the face of adversity. For example, one might create an if-then plan such as "If it's raining outside, then I will walk on the treadmill at the gym instead of going to the park."

Several studies have demonstrated the effectiveness of goal-setting and implementation intentions for enhancing willpower and promoting behavior change. These strategies have been shown to increase motivation, improve self-regulation, and foster a sense of personal control over one's actions. By adopting these techniques, individuals can develop a proactive mindset to overcome obstacles and persevere in pursuing their goals.

Incorporating goal-setting and implementation intentions into daily life can profoundly impact one's ability to harness willpower and achieve desired outcomes. These strategies provide a structured framework for translating intentions into actions and help individuals remain focused and committed to facing challenges. By adopting these techniques, individuals can cultivate greater self-discipline and resilience, paving the way for lasting success in all areas of life.

In the early 2000s, a young woman named Sarah Johnson found herself in a difficult place in life. Struggling with her weight, self-esteem, and professional aspirations, she felt lost and overwhelmed. She knew she needed to make a change, but she didn't know where to start. It wasn't until she came across the power of goal-setting and implementation intentions that her life began to transform.

Sarah first learned about goal setting and implementation intentions through a self-help book she picked up on a whim. Intrigued by the potential benefits of these techniques, she decided to try them. She set a specific, measurable, achievable, relevant, and time-bound (SMART) goal: to lose 50 pounds in a year. This goal provided her with a clear direction and timeframe to achieve it.

To make her goal more manageable, Sarah broke it down into smaller milestones, such as losing five pounds per month. This made the task less daunting and allowed her to celebrate small victories along the way. She also set specific goals for her exercise and diet, such as walking for 30 minutes five times a week and limiting her daily calorie intake.

Next, Sarah developed implementation intentions to ensure she would follow through on her commitments. She created an "if-then" plan for her exercise routine, stating, "If it's a weekday morning at 6:00 AM, then I will go for a 30-minute walk in the park." This level of specificity made it easier for her to integrate exercise into her daily routine and increased her chances of success.

Sarah also identified potential obstacles that could derail her progress, such as her love for sweet treats and her tendency to skip workouts when feeling tired. To address these challenges, she created additional "if-then" plans. For instance, "If I crave something sweet, then I will have a piece of fruit instead of a cookie," and "If I feel too tired to exercise, then I will walk for at least 15 minutes to boost my energy."

As Sarah began to implement her plans, she started to see results. The weight began to come off, and her confidence grew. She began to share her journey on social media, documenting her progress, challenges, and victories. Her story resonated with others facing similar struggles, and she soon amassed a large following of supporters who cheered her on and offered encouragement.

Sarah's success with her weight loss goal inspired her to tackle other areas of her life. She set a new SMART goal to advance her career, aiming to earn a promotion within two years. Using the same strategies that had helped her achieve her weight loss goal, she created an action plan that included taking on more responsibilities at work, attending professional development courses, and networking with key individuals in her industry.

Over time, Sarah's dedication and commitment to her goals paid off. Not only did she successfully lose 50 pounds, but she also earned the promotion she had been working toward. Her story became a testament to the power of goal setting and implementation intentions, proving that anyone can harness their willpower and achieve remarkable success with the right strategies.

Sarah's journey was featured on a popular news website, which further amplified her story and inspired countless others to take control of their lives.

Her story demonstrated the transformative power of goal setting and implementation intentions, showing that these strategies can be applied to virtually any area of life, from weight loss and career advancement to personal relationships and personal development.

Today, Sarah continues to use goal-setting and implementation intentions to pursue her dreams and maintain her healthy lifestyle. She is a living example of the power of these techniques. Her story reminds us that anyone can overcome obstacles and achieve their goals with determination, self-discipline, and the right tools.

8.3 The Power of Visualization and Affirmations

Visualization and affirmations are powerful techniques that help individuals enhance their willpower and achieve their goals. Visualization involves creating vivid mental images of desired outcomes, while affirmations are positive statements that help to reframe one's mindset and instill a sense of self-belief.

Research has shown that visualization can activate the same neural pathways used when performing a task, making it a valuable tool for improving performance, building confidence, and increasing motivation. By consistently visualizing themselves as achieving their goals, individuals can prime their brains for success and make it more likely that they will take the necessary steps to reach their objectives.

Conversely, affirmations work by replacing negative thoughts and self-doubt with positive, empowering beliefs. By regularly repeating affirmations, individuals can rewire their brains, strengthen their belief in their abilities, and boost their self-esteem. This, in turn, can help them overcome challenges and persevere in the face of adversity, both of which are essential for maintaining willpower.

To effectively use visualization and affirmations, practicing these techniques consistently and intentionally is essential. When visualizing, individuals should create detailed mental images of their desired outcomes, engaging all of their senses and imagining the feelings and emotions associated with achieving their goals. This helps create a strong emotional connection to the goal, which is highly motivating.

When creating affirmations, individuals should focus on crafting positive, present-tense statements that reflect the qualities and outcomes they wish to cultivate. These affirmations should be personal, meaningful, and tailored to the individual's goals and circumstances. For example, someone working on improving their self-discipline might claim, "I am focused, disciplined, and in control of my actions."

By incorporating visualization and affirmations into their daily routines, individuals can strengthen their willpower and increase their likelihood of achieving their goals. These techniques can be instrumental when faced with setbacks or obstacles, as they can help to restore motivation and maintain a positive mindset.

In sports, the power of visualization and affirmations has been well-documented, helping numerous athletes achieve success against all odds. One such inspirational story is that of the British cyclist Sir Chris Hoy.

Sir Chris Hoy, born in 1976 in Edinburgh, Scotland, had a passion for cycling from an early age. He began competitive cycling at 14, and by the time he reached his early twenties, Hoy was already making a name for himself in the sport. However, he faced numerous challenges and setbacks throughout his career, including injuries and disappointing performances.

Hoy turned to the power of visualization and affirmations to overcome these obstacles. He would spend hours visualizing himself winning races, picturing every detail of the race, including the feel of the bike beneath him, the wind in his face, and the crowd's roar as he crossed the finish line. He also used affirmations, repeating positive statements to himself, such as "I am strong," "I am fast," and "I am a winner."

Hoy's dedication to visualization and affirmations began to pay off. In the 2004 Athens Olympics, he won his first gold medal in the 1km time trial event. This success fueled his determination, and he continued to use these mental techniques to enhance his performance.

In preparation for the 2008 Beijing Olympics, Hoy ramped up his visualization practice. He focused on his own performance and studied his competitors closely, visualizing how he would react to their moves and strategies during the race. His affirmations also became more specific, tailored to each event he participated in.

Hoy's hard work and mental preparation paid off spectacularly at the Beijing Olympics. He won three gold medals in the Keirin, Team Sprint, and Individual Sprint events, becoming the first Briton in a hundred years to achieve such a feat. His incredible success earned him a knighthood in 2009.

Following his achievements in Beijing, Hoy continued to use visualization and affirmations to maintain his competitive edge. He set his sights on the 2012 London Olympics and began visualizing himself winning gold in front of his home crowd.

In London, Hoy was good. He claimed two more gold medals in the Keirin and Team Sprint events, making him the most decorated British Olympian then, with six gold medals and one silver.

Even after retiring from professional cycling in 2013, Hoy has continued to speak about the importance of visualization and affirmations in achieving success. He credits these mental techniques with helping him overcome challenges and maintain focus during his career.

In the world of entertainment, the power of visualization and affirmations has also significantly impacted the lives and careers of many successful individuals. One such remarkable story is that of the renowned comedian and actor Jim Carrey.

Born in Newmarket, Ontario, Canada, in 1962, Jim Carrey faced a difficult childhood marked by financial instability and personal struggles. At 15, he had to balance his education with a full-time job as a janitor to help support his family. Despite the hardships, Carrey dreamed of becoming a successful actor and comedian.

Carrey turned to visualization and affirmations to keep his spirits up and focus on his dreams. He would spend time each day imagining himself as a successful actor, performing in front of large audiences and receiving praise from fans and critics alike. He also used positive affirmations, repeating phrases such as "I am talented," "I am funny," and "I am destined for success."

As Carrey worked to establish himself in the entertainment industry, he continued to practice visualization and affirmations. In the early 1990s, his career took off with roles in popular television shows and movies, such as "In Living Color," "Ace Ventura: Pet Detective," and "The Mask."

In 1995, Carrey shared a famous story about the power of visualization in his life. While struggling to find acting work, he wrote himself a check for 10 million dollars, dated it for five years in the future, and added the memo "for acting services rendered." He then visualized himself receiving such a sum for his acting work.

In November 1995, just before the five-year deadline, Carrey received a movie role that paid him exactly 10 million dollars. This remarkable coincidence highlights the power of visualization and its role in his success.

Throughout his career, Carrey continued to use visualization and affirmations to maintain his motivation and achieve his goals. His success in comedy and drama and his ability to reinvent himself as an actor can be attributed partly to his unwavering belief in his abilities and the power of his mind.

Now let's put them together.

Imagine enhancing willpower as if cultivating a thriving, lush garden within the landscape of our minds. Each strategy we use to strengthen our willpower represents a unique and essential element that contributes to the garden's growth, enabling it to flourish and thrive.

Mindfulness and meditation serve as the fertile soil in which the garden is rooted, providing a stable and nurturing foundation for our willpower to grow. As we practice mindfulness and meditation, we cultivate a deeper awareness of our thoughts and emotions, nourishing the seeds of our willpower and enabling them to take root in our minds.

Goal setting and implementation intentions are like the trellises and support structures that give our willpower direction and purpose, guiding its growth toward the sunlight. With clear goals and actionable steps, our willpower climbs confidently, reaching for the sky and blossoming into its full potential.

The power of visualization and affirmations is akin to the life-giving sunlight that fuels the growth and vitality of our garden. By visualizing our success and reinforcing our beliefs with positive affirmations, we infuse our willpower with the energy and motivation needed to thrive, allowing it to bask in the warmth of our unwavering belief in our abilities.

When these strategies come together harmoniously, they create a garden of willpower that flourishes within our minds and produces a bountiful harvest of resilience, determination, and self-control. Through the nurturing combination of mindfulness and meditation, goal setting and implementation intentions, and visualization and affirmations, we can tend to our mental garden and reap the rewards of robust and resilient willpower.

Chapter 9: Overcoming Willpower Fatigue

9.1 Recognizing and Managing Ego Depletion

Willpower, like a muscle, can become fatigued and weakened after continuous exertion. This phenomenon is known as ego depletion, a term coined by psychologist Roy Baumeister. Ego depletion is the decline in self-control and willpower that occurs after an individual has engaged in multiple, successive acts of self-regulation. When willpower is exhausted, individuals become more susceptible to indulging in impulsive behaviors and making poor decisions.

Recognizing the signs of ego depletion is essential in managing and overcoming willpower fatigue. Some common symptoms include irritability, increased procrastination, impulsive decision-making, and difficulty maintaining focus. By being aware of these warning signs, individuals can take steps to replenish their willpower reserves before they hit rock bottom.

One effective method to combat ego depletion is prioritizing tasks requiring the most self-control and willpower. Tackling these tasks earlier in the day, when willpower is at its peak, can help prevent the detrimental effects of ego depletion later on. Additionally, regular daily breaks to engage in activities promoting relaxation and mental restoration can replenish willpower reserves.

Another strategy for managing ego depletion is implementing habits and routines that minimize the need for constant self-control. Individuals can preserve their willpower for more important tasks and decisions by automating certain aspects of daily life. For instance, establishing a set morning routine can eliminate the need for willpower-intensive decision-making early in the day.

It is also crucial to fuel the body with proper nutrition, as glucose levels have been linked to willpower and self-control. A balanced diet rich in whole foods can help maintain stable blood sugar levels and support sustained willpower throughout the day.

Lastly, individuals should be aware of the power of sleep in replenishing willpower reserves. Adequate rest is vital for mental and physical well-being and can significantly impact one's ability to exercise self-control and maintain focus.

Once there was a celebrity who faced numerous challenges and setbacks throughout her career. Born into a low-income family, she had to battle adversity from a young age, but her unwavering determination helped her rise above her circumstances. This is the story of Jennifer Lopez, a highly successful actress, singer, dancer, and entrepreneur, who has managed to maintain her willpower and achieve incredible success despite the odds stacked against her.

Jennifer's journey began in the Bronx, New York, where she was born and raised. Growing up, she had a passion for dance and music, which led her to join her school's musical theater program. Her parents, however, did not entirely support her dreams, fearing that an entertainment career would not provide financial stability. This opposition only fueled Jennifer's desire to prove them wrong and to succeed in her chosen path.

Early in her career, Jennifer understood the importance of conserving her willpower and managing ego depletion. She prioritized her tasks, focusing on the most important ones earlier in the day when her willpower was at its highest. This approach allowed her to be highly productive and make significant progress in her career.

Jennifer also recognized the importance of establishing routines and habits to minimize the need for constant self-control. She maintained a strict daily routine, including waking up early, exercising, practicing her craft, and spending time with family and friends. This structure helped her conserve her willpower for more significant tasks and decisions.

To further combat ego depletion, Jennifer practiced self-care by nourishing her body with a balanced diet and getting sufficient sleep. She understood the impact of proper nutrition on her willpower reserves. She made it a point to consume nutrient-dense, whole foods to maintain stable blood sugar levels throughout the day. Additionally, she prioritized rest and sleep, recognizing their importance in replenishing her willpower and keeping her focus.

Jennifer also made a conscious effort to take regular breaks and engage in activities that promoted relaxation and mental restoration. She enjoyed spending time outdoors, meditating, and practicing yoga, which allowed her to recharge her mental batteries and avoid willpower fatigue.

Jennifer faced numerous challenges and setbacks as her career progressed, including failed relationships, box office flops, and negative media attention. Despite these obstacles, she did not succumb to willpower fatigue. Instead, she practiced self-compassion and forgiveness, acknowledging her mistakes and using them as learning opportunities to grow and improve.

Jennifer also understood the importance of balancing work, rest, and play. She made time for leisure activities and socializing with friends and family, knowing that maintaining this balance was crucial for preventing burnout and preserving her willpower.

Throughout her career, Jennifer has demonstrated a remarkable ability to bounce back from adversity and continue pursuing her goals with unwavering determination. Her success can be attributed, in large part, to her skillful management of willpower and her ability to overcome willpower fatigue.

The Radish Experiment, conducted by Roy Baumeister and his colleagues in 1998, is a famous psychological experiment demonstrating the concept of ego depletion and the effects of willpower fatigue. In this study, participants were randomly assigned to one of two conditions - the radish or chocolate conditions.

The researchers set up a room with a table containing a plate of freshly baked cookies and a bowl of radishes. The room was intentionally filled with the aroma of the baked cookies to make the situation more tempting. Participants in the radish condition were instructed to eat only radishes, while those in the chocolate condition were allowed to eat the cookies. The participants were left alone in the room for a few minutes, during which the researchers observed their behavior through a one-way mirror.

Participants in the radish condition had to resist the temptation to eat the cookies and exert self-control, leading to the depletion of their willpower resources. After the initial task, participants were asked to complete a second, seemingly unrelated task - solving a series of complex and unsolvable geometric puzzles.

The researchers measured each participant's time trying to solve the puzzles before giving up. This served as a measure of their persistence and remaining willpower. The experiment results showed that participants in the radish condition, who had to resist the temptation of eating cookies, spent significantly less time attempting to solve the puzzles than those in the chocolate condition. This suggested that the participants in the radish condition had depleted their willpower resources while resisting the cookies, leaving them with less willpower to persist in the puzzle task.

The findings of the Radish Experiment support the concept of ego depletion and demonstrate that exerting self-control can lead to a temporary depletion of willpower resources, resulting in reduced persistence and performance in subsequent tasks. The Radish Experiment highlights the importance of recognizing and managing ego depletion to conserve willpower and maintain optimal performance. By understanding the limits of our willpower and implementing strategies to replenish it, such as taking breaks, practicing self-compassion, and engaging in restorative activities, we can avoid willpower fatigue and perform at our best.

9.2 Self-Compassion and Forgiveness

Self-compassion and forgiveness play a vital role in overcoming willpower fatigue and maintaining a healthy level of self-control. Self-compassion means treating ourselves with kindness, understanding, and patience, even when we fail or make mistakes. It involves acknowledging that we are human and imperfections are a natural part of the human experience.

Research has shown that individuals who practice self-compassion tend to have greater emotional resilience, better mental health, and higher overall well-being. Self-compassion can act as a buffer against negative emotions, such as shame, guilt, and self-criticism, which can undermine our willpower and lead to a vicious cycle of self-defeating behaviors.

Forgiveness, both of oneself and others, is another essential aspect of self-compassion. Holding onto grudges, resentment, or feelings of guilt can be emotionally draining and can further deplete our willpower resources. Forgiving ourselves for our mistakes and shortcomings allows us to let go of negative emotions, conserve willpower, and focus on moving forward positively and constructively.

Practicing self-compassion and forgiveness can be done through various techniques, such as mindfulness meditation, journaling, or engaging in self-care activities that promote relaxation and well-being. By incorporating these practices into our daily routines, we can cultivate a kinder and more understanding relationship with ourselves, which can ultimately help us overcome willpower fatigue and enhance our self-control.

In addition to their benefits, self-compassion and forgiveness can also support one another in reinforcing a positive mindset. When we forgive ourselves for our mistakes, we are more likely to treat ourselves with kindness and understanding, further nurturing self-compassion. Similarly, when we practice self-compassion, we become more open to forgiving ourselves and others, recognizing that we all experience challenges and setbacks.

Embracing self-compassion and forgiveness can create a more supportive inner environment that enables us to manage our willpower resources better and maintain self-control, even when faced with adversity or setbacks. Developing these qualities enhances our ability to overcome willpower fatigue and foster personal growth, resilience, and a more profound sense of well-being.

Kevin Love, an accomplished basketball player, had already achieved significant success in the NBA, including winning a championship with the Cleveland Cavaliers in 2016. Despite these achievements, Love dealt with various mental health challenges, including anxiety and depression.

In November 2017, during a game against the Atlanta Hawks, Love experienced a panic attack. The severity of the attack forced him to leave the game abruptly, which led to widespread speculation and rumors about his sudden exit. Initially, Love felt ashamed of his panic attack and hesitated to disclose why he departed from the game.

However, after seeking therapy and realizing the importance of addressing his mental health, Love opened up about his experiences. In March 2018, he published a personal essay on The Players' Tribune, detailing his struggles with anxiety, depression, and the panic attack that had forced him out of the game. Love expressed the importance of self-compassion and forgiveness in his journey to better mental health and overcoming willpower fatigue.

His decision to share his story resonated with many individuals, both inside and outside the world of professional sports. It also sparked a broader conversation about the importance of mental health awareness and support, particularly among male athletes who might feel pressure to adhere to traditional notions of masculinity and avoid discussing emotional challenges.

As Love continued to work on his mental health, he began incorporating various self-care practices into his daily routine, such as mindfulness meditation, journaling, and regular therapy sessions. He also prioritized sleep, nutrition, and physical exercise to maintain a healthy balance in his life.

Through his ongoing journey, Kevin Love has become an advocate for mental health awareness. He established the Kevin Love Fund in 2018 to provide resources and support for people struggling with mental health challenges. Love's willingness to be open about his struggles and his commitment to self-compassion and forgiveness has allowed him to overcome willpower fatigue and inspire many people facing similar challenges.

Abraham Lincoln, the 16th President of the United States, is known for his exceptional leadership during one of the most tumultuous times in American history. However, behind his remarkable achievements, Lincoln's practice of self-compassion and forgiveness played a crucial role in overcoming willpower fatigue, personal challenges, and political setbacks.

One of the most striking examples of Lincoln's self-compassion can be seen in his handling of personal loss. In 1850, Lincoln's beloved son, Edward, passed away at four. In the face of this unimaginable grief, Lincoln found solace in poetry, particularly the works of William Knox. He often recited Knox's poem "Mortality," which spoke to the fragility of life and the need for self-compassion in times of sorrow.

Lincoln's self-compassion was also evident during his political career, which was marked by defeats and setbacks. In 1858, Lincoln lost the Illinois Senate race to Stephen A. Douglas. However, Lincoln remained determined and focused on the future instead of wallowing in self-pity or giving up.

In a letter to a friend, he wrote, "The fight must go on. The cause of civil liberty must not be surrendered at the end of one or even one hundred defeats."

This mindset showcases Lincoln's ability to practice self-compassion and forgiveness in the face of failure, ultimately leading to his election as President two years later.

As a leader, Lincoln extended his practice of self-compassion and forgiveness to others. One famous example is his relationship with his former rival, William H. Seward. After defeating Seward for the Republican nomination in 1860, Lincoln surprised many by offering him the position of Secretary of State. This act of forgiveness and inclusion set the tone for Lincoln's administration, characterized by a spirit of cooperation and unity.

Lincoln's ability to forgive was also demonstrated in his response to the Civil War. In his second inaugural address, he urged the nation to move forward "with malice toward none, with charity for all." This call for unity and forgiveness, even in the face of enormous suffering and division, is a testament to Lincoln's deep understanding of the importance of self-compassion and forgiveness in overcoming willpower fatigue.

In summary, Abraham Lincoln's life and leadership offer numerous examples of the power of self-compassion and forgiveness in overcoming challenges and setbacks. His ability to practice these virtues in adversity inspires those facing their struggles. It illustrates the crucial role of self-compassion and forgiveness in overcoming willpower fatigue.

9.3 Balancing Work, Rest, and Play

Achieving a balance between work, rest, and play is essential for maintaining and enhancing willpower. Striking the right balance prevents burnout and exhaustion, allowing individuals to pursue their goals with sustained energy and focus. When people allocate sufficient time for leisure activities and relaxation, they can replenish their mental and emotional reserves, ultimately supporting their willpower and overall well-being.

An essential component of maintaining this balance is ensuring that individuals take regular breaks during workdays. Studies have shown periodic breaks increase productivity, creativity, and problem-solving skills. These breaks allow one to step back from the task and gain a fresh perspective, potentially leading to new insights and ideas.

Sufficient sleep is another crucial aspect of balancing work, rest, and play. Sleep deprivation can impair cognitive functions, emotional regulation, and decision-making abilities, all of which are essential components of willpower. Ensuring one gets adequate restorative sleep allows the brain to recharge and recover, supporting optimal willpower and functioning throughout the day.

Furthermore, engaging in leisure activities and hobbies can provide a much-needed respite from work and everyday life demands. These activities can help reduce stress, promote relaxation, and enhance overall well-being. Incorporating enjoyable activities into one's daily routine makes it easier to maintain motivation and willpower over the long term.

Creating a supportive social network balances work, rest, and play. Connecting with friends and family can provide emotional support, encouragement, and a sense of belonging. These connections can help buffer against the negative effects of stress and contribute to increased resilience and willpower.

In the world of high-performance athletics, athletes need to maintain a balance between work, rest, and play to achieve their goals. The renowned tennis champion Roger Federer is one such athlete who has mastered this balance. Federer's career has spanned over two decades, during which he has consistently remained at the top of the game. His ability to sustain such a high level of performance for an extended period is attributed to his commitment to balancing work, rest, and play.

Federer has always been committed to his training and practice routines as a professional athlete. However, unlike many peers who focus solely on their sport, Federer has prioritized balancing his work with relaxation and leisure activities. This approach has allowed him to maintain a fresh perspective on his career, reducing the risk of burnout and enhancing his overall well-being.

One key aspect of Federer's strategy for achieving balance is his approach to taking breaks from the competition. Throughout his career, he has strategically scheduled breaks during the tennis season to allow himself to rest and recharge mentally and physically. These breaks have been significant as Federer has gotten older, allowing him to continue competing at the highest level well into his 30s.

In addition to scheduling breaks during the season, Federer has diligently ensured he gets enough sleep.

He has often spoken about the importance of sleep for optimal performance, noting that he aims for at least eight hours of sleep per night. This commitment to rest has helped Federer maintain his mental sharpness and physical resilience on the court.

Federer's dedication to leisure and hobbies has also played a significant role in his ability to maintain balance. An avid fan of sports like soccer and basketball, he enjoys engaging in these activities during his downtime. Additionally, Federer is passionate about travel and often combines his love for exploration with his professional commitments, visiting various destinations on the ATP tour.

Another important aspect of Federer's balanced lifestyle is his commitment to spending time with his family. Married with four children, he has always prioritized his family life, even when it requires him to make sacrifices in his career. This focus on the family has provided Federer with a strong support system and a source of motivation, helping him maintain his willpower and drive for success.

In 2017, Federer made a remarkable comeback after a six-month break from tennis due to a knee injury. Many believed his career was nearing its end, but Federer's commitment to balancing work, rest, and play allowed him to return to the sport reinvigorated. He went on to win two Grand Slam titles that year, proving that his approach to maintaining balance was crucial to his continued success.

The following year, in 2018, Federer became the oldest world number one in tennis history. This achievement further reinforced the importance of his approach to balancing work, rest, and play. By prioritizing self-care and maintaining a well-rounded lifestyle, Federer defied the odds and achieved remarkable success.

Federer's success story is a testament to the power of balancing work, rest, and play. His approach has enabled him to maintain high performance on the court and enjoy a fulfilling life off the court.

Chapter 10: Willpower and Personal Growth

10.1 Developing a Growth Mindset

A growth mindset is a key factor in personal growth, as it enables individuals to view challenges and setbacks as opportunities for learning and improvement. When people adopt a growth mindset, they believe their abilities can be developed through hard work, dedication, and resilience. This contrasts with a fixed mindset, where individuals believe their abilities are innate and unchangeable. Developing a growth mindset can significantly enhance willpower, encouraging individuals to persevere in the face of obstacles and strive for constant self-improvement.

To develop a growth mindset, embracing the idea that skills and abilities can be cultivated and enhanced over time is essential. This requires a shift in focus from solely measuring success by outcomes to valuing the process of learning and personal development. By appreciating the journey and recognizing the incremental progress made along the way, individuals with a growth mindset are more likely to maintain their willpower in the face of challenges.

One crucial aspect of cultivating a growth mindset is viewing failure as a valuable learning opportunity. Instead of seeing setbacks as evidence of personal shortcomings, individuals with a growth mindset perceive them as opportunities to learn, adapt, and grow. This perspective enables them to bounce back from failure with renewed determination and willpower, continually seeking ways to improve and progress.

Another important element in developing a growth mindset is embracing the power of effort. Recognizing that effort is the key to improvement encourages individuals to take on challenges and push their limits. When faced with difficult tasks, those with a growth mindset are more likely to exert the necessary willpower to overcome obstacles, as they understand that success results from hard work and perseverance.

Fostering a growth mindset requires cultivating curiosity and a love for learning. This involves seeking new experiences and knowledge, actively pursuing personal development, and embracing change. With this mindset, individuals are better equipped to adapt to new situations, maintain their willpower in uncertainty, and continuously evolve and grow.

One of the most famous experiments illustrating the concept of a growth mindset was conducted by Dr. Carol Dweck, a renowned psychologist and author of the book "Mindset: The New Psychology of Success." This groundbreaking study explored the impact of different mindsets on students' motivation and achievement.

The experiment began by selecting a group of students in a middle school setting. These students were divided into two groups at random, with the only distinction between the groups being the type of feedback they would receive. The first group, the "fixed mindset" group, was given praise focused on their intelligence, while the second group, the "growth mindset" group, received praise for their effort and hard work.

Dweck and her team carefully observed their behavior and reactions to success and failure as the students progressed through challenging tasks. They found that students in the fixed mindset group quickly became discouraged when faced with difficult tasks. As their intelligence had been praised, they perceived failure as a reflection of their inherent lack of ability. Consequently, these students were more likely to give up and avoid challenges in the future, fearing that failure would reveal their inadequacy.

In contrast, the students in the growth mindset group demonstrated remarkable resilience when faced with the same challenges. They embraced the difficulties as opportunities to learn and grow, not threats to their self-worth. When they encountered setbacks, they responded with increased determination and persistence, motivated by the belief that their efforts would lead to improvement.

As the study continued, Dweck and her team introduced more complex tasks, which provided further opportunities for the students to demonstrate their growth or fixed mindset behaviors. They found that the students in the growth mindset group were more likely to ask for help and seek feedback when faced with obstacles, as they understood that this would facilitate their learning and development. On the other hand, the students in the fixed mindset group were more likely to avoid seeking assistance, fearing that doing so would expose their perceived lack of ability.

The results of this study were striking, as they revealed the significant impact of mindset on motivation and achievement. The students in the growth mindset group outperformed their fixed mindset peers in various measures, including problem-solving skills, persistence, and academic performance.

The implications of this experiment extend far beyond the classroom setting. In professional and personal contexts, individuals with a growth mindset are more likely to embrace challenges, persevere in the face of setbacks, and seek opportunities for growth and development.

Dr. Dweck's research has inspired countless subsequent studies exploring the impact of mindset on a wide range of domains, from sports performance to professional success. A growth mindset has become a cornerstone of modern psychology, influencing educational practices, coaching strategies, and personal development approaches worldwide.

Sara Blakely, the founder of the billion-dollar company Spanx, is an outstanding example of someone who embraced a growth mindset on her path to success. Her story has been featured in various news outlets and serves as an inspiration to many.

Growing up, Blakely was no stranger to failure. Her father encouraged her and her brother to celebrate their failures, believing failures were simply opportunities to learn and grow. This unconventional upbringing instilled in Blakely the belief that there was no shame in making mistakes as long as she learned from them and kept moving forward.

After graduating from college, Blakely held various sales jobs, including one where she sold fax machines door-to-door. One day, while getting dressed for a party, she realized she didn't have the proper undergarments under her white pants. This led her to cut the feet off a pair of pantyhose, and the idea for Spanx was born.

Despite having no background in fashion or design, Blakely was determined to turn her idea into reality. She faced countless rejections and setbacks, but her growth mindset empowered her to persist. She took on the challenge of learning everything she could about the hosiery industry, even going as far as researching pantyhose patents at the library.

Blakely's perseverance paid off when she finally found a manufacturer willing to take a chance on her idea. She then strategically sent samples of her product to celebrities and influential people, hoping they would endorse and popularize her brand. Oprah Winfrey, one of the recipients, featured Spanx on her show, which boosted the company's sales exponentially.

Even after achieving success, Blakely continued learning and growing. She continued to expand her product line, focusing on innovating and improving her offerings. Today, Spanx is a global brand, and Blakely is one of the world's most successful self-made female entrepreneurs.

Sara Blakely's story demonstrates the power of a growth mindset in overcoming challenges and achieving success. Her willingness to learn from her failures, embrace the unknown, and persist in the face of adversity ultimately led her to create a billion-dollar company. Blakely's journey serves as a reminder that adopting a growth mindset can unlock untold potential and turn even the most far-fetched dreams into reality.

10.2 The Role of Willpower in Achievement and Success

The role of willpower in achievement and success cannot be overstated. Willpower is the driving force that enables individuals to stay focused, persevere through obstacles, and maintain the discipline necessary to achieve their goals. It is a vital component of personal growth and development and can significantly impact one's chances of success in various aspects of life.

One of the main ways willpower contributes to achievement and success is by helping individuals maintain consistency and discipline in their efforts. Character is critical in achieving long-term goals, as it helps create sustainable progress. Willpower fuels the ability to resist short-term temptations or distractions and stay committed to one's goals, even when faced with adversity or setbacks.

Willpower also plays a crucial role in managing and overcoming procrastination, a common obstacle to success. Procrastination can hinder progress by causing individuals to delay or avoid taking action on essential tasks. By developing strong willpower, individuals can overcome the urge to procrastinate and take consistent action toward their goals, making it more likely that they will achieve success.

In addition, willpower can help individuals develop resilience, which is essential for success in the face of challenges and adversity. Resilience is the ability to bounce back from setbacks and adapt to changing circumstances. Strong willpower enables individuals to maintain their focus and motivation during difficult times, allowing them to continue working toward their goals despite their challenges.

Willpower can play a significant role in personal growth and self-improvement. By exerting willpower to develop new habits, learn new skills, or break old patterns, individuals can make lasting changes that contribute to their overall success and well-being. This personal growth can lead to increased self-confidence, better decision-making, and improved problem-solving abilities, all of which can contribute to tremendous success in various aspects of life.

Garrett Morgan's story weaves a narrative of resilience and determination in adversity. Born in 1877 in Claysville, Kentucky, Garrett was the son of formerly enslaved people. Growing up, he had limited access to education, attending school only through the fifth grade. Undeterred by this, he was determined to succeed and make a difference.

As a young teenager, Morgan left home and moved to Cincinnati, Ohio, in search of better opportunities. He worked as a handyman to support himself while also pursuing his education. Morgan was relentless in his quest for knowledge and self-improvement. He read extensively, attended night school, and sought the mentorship of a local businessman.

His dedication and hard work eventually led him to Cleveland, Ohio, where he established his own sewing machine and shoe repair shop. Morgan's innovative mindset pushed him to invent a belt fastener for sewing machines, which he sold to the market, earning him a small fortune. This success allowed him to expand his business interests into newspaper publishing and automobile sales.

However, it was his passion for inventing that truly set Morgan apart. In 1914, he created the "safety hood," a device that would later evolve into the modern gas mask. This invention proved critical during World War I, saving countless lives in the trenches of Europe. Morgan's gas mask was also used by firefighters, enabling them to enter smoke-filled buildings and rescue those trapped inside.

In 1923, Morgan once again showcased his innovative spirit by inventing the three-position traffic signal, which helped to control the growing chaos of automobile traffic in urban areas. This invention was the first of its kind in the United States and played a crucial role in establishing traffic management systems that we still use today.

Morgan's life was not without challenges. As an African American, he faced many obstacles during racial segregation and discrimination in his pursuit of success. Yet, his willpower and determination allowed him to persevere and overcome these barriers.

For instance, when Morgan attempted to market his safety hood, he encountered resistance due to his race. Rather than giving up, he hired a white actor to pose as the inventor during demonstrations while Morgan donned the device and entered hazardous situations to prove its effectiveness.

Garrett Morgan's unwavering commitment to his dreams and his ability to rise above societal limitations serve as a powerful testament to the role of willpower in achievement and success. His inventions and entrepreneurial spirit significantly impacted society, and his legacy inspires others.

Throughout his life, Morgan demonstrated an insatiable curiosity and a drive to learn, adapt, and innovate. He embodied that anyone can achieve greatness through hard work, persistence, and belief in oneself, regardless of background or circumstances.

Ultimately, Garrett Morgan's story is an inspiring example of the power of willpower and its role in personal achievement and success. His determination and unwavering commitment to his dreams allowed him to overcome barriers and make a lasting impact on the world.

10.3 Fostering Lifelong Learning and Adaptability

Lifelong learning and adaptability are crucial to personal growth and success, especially in today's rapidly changing world. Fostering a mindset of continuous learning and being open to new experiences are essential for maintaining personal and professional relevance. Moreover, they can significantly enhance an individual's willpower as they contribute to increased self-awareness, self-efficacy, and resilience.

Fostering lifelong learning and adaptability begins with cultivating a growth mindset. A growth mindset believes one's abilities and intelligence can be developed through hard work, dedication, and learning from experiences. This perspective encourages individuals to embrace challenges, persevere through setbacks, and view failures as opportunities for growth and improvement. In contrast, a fixed mindset assumes that abilities and intelligence are static, leading to a reluctance to take on challenges and a fear of failure.

A growth mindset can be encouraged by setting realistic yet challenging goals, seeking personal and professional development opportunities, and embracing a curious and open-minded attitude. Developing strong problem-solving skills and the ability to adapt and thrive in the face of adversity is also essential.

One way to promote lifelong learning is to engage in activities stimulating personal and intellectual growth. This could include reading widely, attending workshops and seminars, participating in online courses, or joining clubs and organizations that align with one's interests and passions. Engaging with others who share similar goals and aspirations can also be an excellent source of motivation and support.

It is crucial to recognize the value of experiential learning, which refers to acquiring knowledge and skills through direct experience. This could involve immersing oneself in new environments, taking on challenging projects, or pursuing personal passions outside of work or education. Such experiences can provide valuable insights and foster adaptability by exposing individuals to different perspectives and ways of thinking.

Cultivating a sense of self-compassion and self-forgiveness is essential for fostering lifelong learning and adaptability. It is vital to accept that setbacks and failures are inevitable parts of personal growth and that learning from these experiences is more important than avoiding them. Acknowledging one's limitations and being kind to oneself in the face of challenges can significantly boost resilience and willpower.

Benjamin Banneker, an African American scientist, mathematician, and astronomer, is an excellent example of a historical figure who embodied the concept of lifelong learning and adaptability. Born in 1731 in Baltimore County, Maryland, Banneker was a largely self-taught individual who significantly contributed to science and civil rights.

Despite being born into a time when educational opportunities for African Americans were limited, Banneker's curiosity and determination led him to educate himself in various subjects. His early interest in mathematics was sparked when a Quaker family, who believed in the importance of education for all, lent him a mathematics book. Banneker's drive for learning was evident as he absorbed the knowledge from the book and began to apply it to his life.

As Banneker's knowledge grew, he became interested in astronomy. He taught himself the subject by reading books and observing celestial bodies through a borrowed telescope. Using his mathematical skills, he could accurately predict solar eclipses and chart the movement of stars. His passion for learning and adaptability allowed him to excel in a new field.

In addition to his scientific pursuits, Banneker was an active voice in the fight against slavery and racial inequality. He used his intellect and writing skills to advocate for the abolition of slavery and equal rights for all. His correspondence with Thomas Jefferson, then the Secretary of State, included a letter in which Banneker urged him to reconsider his views on race and slavery.

Benjamin Banneker's drive for knowledge extended beyond the realm of science. He was also a skilled inventor and clockmaker. In a remarkable feat of ingenuity, Banneker built a wooden clock that accurately kept time for over 50 years. This accomplishment showcased his mechanical aptitude and ability to learn and adapt to new challenges.

Throughout his life, Banneker continued to seek knowledge and apply it to various areas. His remarkable achievements in science, civil rights, and invention were a testament to his commitment to lifelong learning and adaptability.

Now let's use a fictional story to illustrate how people can use all the concepts above together to serve their purposes.

In the small town of Willowbrook, three friends - Abby, Ben, and Clara - were on a mission to make their dreams a reality. They knew it would take hard work, dedication, and the power of will to achieve their goals.

Abby was an aspiring artist who wanted to be known for her innovative and thought-provoking pieces. On the other hand, Ben was determined to start a successful tech company that would revolutionize how people interact with technology. Clara, a passionate environmentalist, dreamed of leading a nonprofit organization dedicated to conserving the planet for future generations.

The three friends attended a weekly meetup where they shared their progress, setbacks, and insights. One day, they decided to read a book about personal growth and apply its concepts to their journeys.

At the next meetup, Abby excitedly shared how she had been practicing developing a growth mindset. She explained how she had started embracing challenges, learning from her mistakes, and believing in her ability to improve. This mindset helped her create some of her most potent artwork yet. Inspired by Abby's story, Ben and Clara adopted a growth mindset.

The following week, Ben shared his experience with the role of willpower in achievement and success. He realized he needed to be disciplined and focused on building his tech company. By setting clear, attainable goals and breaking them into smaller tasks,

Ben found it easier to maintain his willpower and make progress. Abby and Clara were motivated by Ben's experience and began implementing goal-setting strategies in their endeavors too.

During the next meeting, Clara spoke about fostering lifelong learning and adaptability. She explained that by constantly seeking new knowledge and staying informed about environmental issues, she was able to adapt her strategies and make her nonprofit more effective. Abby and Ben agreed that being open to learning and adapting was crucial for personal growth and success.

As the weeks passed, the friends continued sharing their experiences and supporting each other on their paths. The concepts of growth mindset, willpower, and lifelong learning became integral to their journeys, helping them overcome obstacles and move closer to their goals.

Abby, Ben, and Clara discovered the power of personal growth and the importance of applying these concepts through their interactions. Their shared experiences brought them closer together and allowed them to learn from one another, demonstrating the power of friendship and collaboration in achieving success.

Chapter 11: Willpower in Relationships

11.1 The Role of Willpower in Building and Maintaining Relationships

Relationships are:

- An integral part of human life.
- Encompassing various aspects such as romantic partnerships.
- Friendships.
- Professional connections.

Each relationship is unique and requires effort, dedication, and, most importantly, willpower to prosper. This chapter will examine the importance of willpower in building and maintaining relationships and discuss strategies for cultivating this essential quality.

Willpower, the ability to exert self-control, resist temptation, and persevere during challenging times, is crucial for fostering strong, healthy relationships. It enables individuals to make conscious decisions, act with integrity, and remain committed to the well-being of their relationships. The following sections will explore the various ways in which willpower contributes to the development and preservation of successful relationships:

1. Commitment: Relationships flourish when individuals are dedicated to one another and willing to put forth the necessary effort. Willpower aids in maintaining this commitment, even when faced with obstacles. It enables individuals to prioritize relationships, work through challenges, and resolve conflicts.

2. Communication: Clear, honest communication is essential to the health of any relationship. Willpower is necessary for effective communication, as it involves active listening, empathy, and vulnerability. Strong willpower allows individuals to express their feelings, needs, and desires more effectively while remaining open to the perspectives of others.

3. Conflict resolution: Disagreements and conflicts are natural occurrences in relationships. Willpower facilitates the ability to navigate these difficult situations with patience, understanding, and a focus on finding common ground. By practicing self-control, individuals can avoid impulsive reactions that often lead to further escalation.

4. Personal growth: Successful relationships involve two individuals committed to personal growth and self-improvement. Willpower enables individuals to consistently invest time and effort in their development, which contributes to the overall health and longevity of the relationship.

5. Trust and loyalty: Trust is established over time through consistent and reliable actions. By exercising willpower, individuals can remain true to their word, follow through on promises, and demonstrate loyalty to their partners and friends. This consistency strengthens the foundation of trust that sustains relationships.

6. Adaptability: Life is filled with changes and uncertainties, and relationships must adapt accordingly. Willpower assists individuals in adapting and growing together as they face new challenges, transitions, and phases in their lives. This resilience is crucial for maintaining long-lasting connections.

In the world of celebrities, relationships often crumble under the pressure of fame and public scrutiny. However, David and Victoria Beckham have defied the odds and maintained a strong, lasting bond. Their story exemplifies how willpower can be harnessed to build and sustain a thriving relationship.

The tale of the famous couple began in 1997 when they first met at a charity football match. Victoria, a member of the Spice Girls, was at the height of her fame, while David was making a name for himself as a talented young footballer. Sparks flew, and they soon embarked on a whirlwind romance that captured the world's attention.

As the couple's relationship progressed, they faced numerous challenges that tested their willpower and commitment to one another. They endured long periods of separation due to their demanding careers, with David playing for various football clubs worldwide and Victoria pursuing her music career and the latest fashion.

Despite the distance, the couple demonstrated an unwavering dedication to their relationship. They made it a priority to communicate regularly, using phone calls and video chats to stay connected. This commitment to open communication was vital in helping them maintain their bond, even when they were thousands of miles apart.

In 1999, David and Victoria exchanged vows in a lavish wedding ceremony, solidifying their commitment to one another. They soon started a family, welcoming their first child, Brooklyn, in 1999, Romeo in 2002, Cruz in 2005, and Harper in 2011. The couple has faced their fair share of parenting challenges throughout the years, but they have always prioritized their children's well-being, nurturing a loving and supportive family environment.

As their fame grew, the couple found themselves constantly in the public eye, with every aspect of their lives scrutinized by the media. This level of exposure could have easily driven a wedge between them, but instead, they chose to use their willpower to remain grounded and focused on what truly mattered: their love for each other and their family.

Inevitably, their relationship has not been without its fair share of conflicts and disagreements. However, David and Victoria have consistently demonstrated their ability to navigate these problematic moments gracefully and with understanding. They have shown a willingness to compromise and work together to find solutions, proving that willpower and effective communication are vital ingredients in successful conflict resolution.

Another factor that has contributed to the strength of their relationship is their commitment to personal growth. David and Victoria have evolved throughout their careers, exploring new ventures and nurturing their passions. This shared dedication to self-improvement has helped them grow together as a couple, forging an even stronger bond.

In the face of adversity, David and Victoria Beckham have consistently displayed trust and loyalty toward each other. They have weathered numerous scandals and rumors, always standing by each other's side and presenting a united front. Their unwavering support for one another is a testament to the power of trust in maintaining a healthy relationship.

Adaptability has also been crucial to the longevity of their relationship. As their lives and careers have evolved, David and Victoria have demonstrated an impressive ability to adapt and grow together. They have embraced change and navigated the various transitions in their lives with resilience and grace, reinforcing the importance of willpower in maintaining a lasting connection.

The story of David and Victoria Beckham showcases the remarkable impact of willpower in building and maintaining a strong, enduring relationship. Their dedication to communication, conflict resolution, personal growth, trust, loyalty, and adaptability has allowed them to withstand life's challenges in the public eye and nurture a loving, supportive partnership that has stood the test of time.

11.2 Communication and Conflict Resolution

In the intricate dance of human relationships, the role of willpower in enhancing communication and resolving conflicts is akin to the delicate interplay of rhythm and movement. By understanding and embracing the transformative power of willpower, we can elevate our connections with others, gracefully navigating the complexities that arise from our unique needs, desires, and perspectives.

Willpower, the force that enables us to exercise self-control and persevere through challenges, is a guiding light in communication. When we harness our willpower to engage in open, honest, and empathetic dialogue, we create an atmosphere of trust and mutual understanding. This shared space allows individuals to express themselves authentically and to actively listen to one another, transcending the barriers that often divide us.

To tap into the potential of willpower in communication, we must first cultivate the art of self-awareness. We can better understand the subtle cues guiding our interactions by becoming attuned to our thoughts, feelings, and reactions. This heightened awareness empowers us to approach conversations with intention and mindfulness, fostering a spirit of genuine connection.

In conflict resolution, willpower serves as a compass, guiding us toward solutions that honor the needs and desires of all parties involved. By harnessing our willpower, we can resist the temptation to succumb to impulsive reactions instead of approaching conflicts with patience and understanding.

As we apply willpower to conflict resolution, we learn to balance the delicate dance of assertion and compromise. We become adept at standing up for our beliefs and needs while remaining open to the viewpoints and needs of others. This graceful interplay demonstrates the power of willpower in fostering resilience and adaptability within relationships.

Furthermore, willpower fuels our capacity for empathy and emotional intelligence, essential tools in conflict resolution. When we actively practice empathy, we seek to understand the emotions and perspectives of others, transcending our own experiences to connect with them on a deeper level. Emotional intelligence, in turn, equips us with the ability to manage our emotions and respond to the emotions of others constructively.

By harnessing the power of willpower in both communication and conflict resolution, we weave a tapestry of connection that is both strong and resilient. This tapestry, enriched by the colors and textures of our unique experiences, is a testament to our relationships' beauty and strength.

In relationships, willpower is a guiding force that illuminates the path toward more profound understanding, authentic connection, and harmonious coexistence. As we continue exploring the nuances of empathy and emotional intelligence in the following sections, we shall uncover the myriad ways these essential skills can further enrich and sustain our connections with others.

The story of Hollywood actor Hugh Jackman and his wife, Deborra-Lee Furness, demonstrates the use of willpower to enhance communication and resolve conflicts. Their long-lasting marriage, which has spanned over two decades, is an inspiring example of how commitment and dedication can lead to a thriving relationship in the world of show business.

Hugh Jackman, known for his iconic roles such as Wolverine in the X-Men series and his performance in Les Misérables, met Deborra-Lee Furness on the set of the Australian television show, "Correlli," in 1995. Despite the age difference and Jackman's rising stardom, they have maintained a loving and supportive relationship, which they attribute to their strong communication skills and conflict-resolution techniques.

The couple has faced many challenges over the years, including dealing with busy schedules and constant tabloid rumors. However, they have consistently prioritized their relationship and family by using willpower to establish and maintain open lines of communication. For instance, Jackman has mentioned in interviews that they always make time for each other and never spend more than two weeks apart, even with their demanding careers.

Jackman and Furness also practice active listening and express their feelings openly and honestly, which has been crucial in navigating their relationship through difficult times. This dedication to effective communication has helped them build a strong foundation of trust and understanding.

Another aspect of their relationship that highlights the importance of willpower is the couple's approach to conflict resolution. Jackman has shared that they consciously try to stay calm and listen to each other's perspectives when disagreements arise. They understand that emotions can run high during conflicts, and they use willpower to maintain control over their reactions, allowing them to find solutions that work for both of them.

Their commitment to healthily resolving conflicts has undoubtedly contributed to the longevity and success of their relationship. By prioritizing empathy and understanding, Jackman and Furness have grown together and maintained a strong bond, despite the pressures of the entertainment industry.

Benjamin Franklin's early life experiences strengthened his communication skills and his willpower. As a young apprentice printer, he honed his ability to express ideas clearly and effectively. Franklin's experiences with various trades and businesses allowed him to interact with people from diverse backgrounds, developing his talent for understanding and empathizing with others.

In the mid-1700s, as tensions between the American colonies and Britain escalated, Franklin's role as a diplomat brought his communication and conflict-resolution skills to the forefront. He served as a representative of several American colonies in London, where he attempted to negotiate a peaceful resolution to the brewing conflict. Franklin's willingness to engage in open dialogue and seek compromise demonstrated his commitment to resolving disputes through diplomacy and communication.

One of the pivotal moments in Franklin's diplomatic career was his involvement in negotiating the Treaty of Paris in 1783, which ended the Revolutionary War between Britain and the American colonies. As a member of the American delegation, Franklin played a crucial role in the negotiations, utilizing his willpower to maintain a calm and diplomatic demeanor, even in the face of staunch opposition.

During these negotiations, Franklin displayed a remarkable ability to empathize with and understand the perspectives of the opposing party. He recognized the importance of addressing the concerns and needs of the British negotiators while also advocating for the interests of the newly independent United States. His diplomatic approach was instrumental in achieving a favorable outcome for both sides.

Franklin's dedication to open communication was also evident in his personal life. He maintained a vast network of correspondents, exchanging letters with friends, family, and acquaintances worldwide. These correspondences often addressed complex and contentious issues of the time, showcasing Franklin's commitment to understanding different perspectives and fostering respectful dialogue.

Later, Franklin continued to champion the importance of diplomacy and conflict resolution. He served as a delegate to the Constitutional Convention in 1787, where he played a crucial role in shaping the formation of the United States government. His wisdom and ability to mediate disputes among the delegates contributed significantly to the creation of the US Constitution.

Franklin's commitment to communication and conflict resolution was broader than politics and diplomacy. He also advocated for religious tolerance, engaging in discussions and debates on spiritual matters with an open mind and a willingness to consider different beliefs.

Throughout his life, Benjamin Franklin demonstrated an unwavering dedication to enhancing communication and resolving conflicts. His diplomatic efforts during the Revolutionary War, his contributions to the formation of the United States government, and his commitment to open dialogue in both his personal and professional life are testaments to the power of willpower in fostering understanding and unity.

11.3 Practicing Empathy and Emotional Intelligence

The significance of practicing empathy and cultivating emotional intelligence cannot be overstated in a world where our relationships form the very foundation of our lives. These essential skills can transform our connections with others, fostering more profound understanding, stronger bonds, and more fulfilling interactions. It is through empathy and emotional intelligence that we unlock our true potential for compassionate and harmonious coexistence.

Empathy, the ability to understand and share the feelings of others, is a vital component of healthy relationships. By putting ourselves in another's shoes, we can see the world through their eyes, transcending our own experiences to connect with them on a deeper level. This connection fosters a sense of trust, respect, and emotional safety, creating a strong foundation upon which our relationships can flourish.

Emotional intelligence, on the other hand, refers to our ability to recognize, understand, and manage our own emotions, as well as the emotions of others. When we cultivate emotional intelligence, we empower ourselves to navigate the complex landscape of human emotions with grace and finesse, ultimately leading to more effective communication, conflict resolution, and relationship-building.

The benefits of practicing empathy and emotional intelligence are profound and far-reaching. By developing these skills, we can enhance our capacity for compassionate communication, allowing us to express our thoughts and feelings in a way that fosters connection and understanding. This communication paves the way for genuine, authentic relationships in which both parties feel valued and heard.

Moreover, empathy and emotional intelligence play a critical role in conflict resolution. As we hone our ability to understand and manage our emotions, we become better equipped to approach disagreements calmly and rationally. This mindset enables us to consider the perspectives and needs of others, even when our emotions are running high.

When we practice empathy and emotional intelligence, we also develop heightened self-awareness. This self-awareness allows us to recognize and address our own needs, as well as the needs of others, ultimately leading to more balanced and fulfilling relationships.

Here are some valuable tips on how to practice empathy and improve emotional intelligence:

1. Active listening: Pay full attention to the person speaking without interrupting or formulating a response in your mind. This shows that you genuinely care about understanding their feelings and perspectives.

2. Practice non-judgment: Approach conversations and situations with an open mind and refrain from judging others based on your biases or experiences. This will enable you to better empathize with their feelings and emotions.

3. Develop self-awareness: Reflect on your own emotions and reactions to various situations. By understanding yourself better, you can more effectively recognize and manage your emotions and empathize with others.

4. Be present: Focus on the present moment during interactions, avoiding distractions and giving your full attention to the person you are with. This will help you identify subtle emotional cues and foster deeper connections.

5. Observe body language: Pay attention to non-verbal cues, such as facial expressions, gestures, and posture, as they can provide insight into a person's emotions and state of mind.

6. Validate emotions: Acknowledge and validate the emotions of others, even if you don't necessarily agree with their perspective. This creates a safe

environment for open communication and helps build trust.

7. Practice perspective-taking: Put yourself in another person's shoes and consider how they may feel or think. This can help you develop a deeper understanding of their emotions and experiences.

8. Cultivate compassion: Nurture a genuine concern for the well-being of others, and strive to be kind and understanding in your interactions.

9. Respond with empathy: Respond with empathy and understanding rather than reacting defensively or aggressively when faced with a difficult situation or conflict. This can help diffuse tensions and pave the way for constructive dialogue.

10. Develop emotional vocabulary: Learn to accurately identify and express your own emotions, as well as the emotions of others. This can help you communicate more effectively and empathetically.

11. Seek feedback: Ask for feedback from friends, family, and colleagues on how well you're practicing empathy and emotional intelligence. This can help you identify areas for improvement and growth.

12. Continuous learning: Engage in activities that promote emotional intelligence, such as reading books, attending workshops, or practicing mindfulness meditation. Regularly working on these

skills will help you develop and maintain empathy and emotional intelligence.

Nelson Mandela was a sign of hope and unity in a world with a long history of racism and unfairness. As a leader and a peacemaker, Mandela became renowned for his exceptional empathy and emotional intelligence, which he employed to achieve significant tasks and unite a nation.

As a young man, Mandela was an attentive listener, always eager to learn from others and hear their stories. He would sit for hours, conversing with people from all walks of life, understanding their struggles and finding common ground. His ability to listen without judgment allowed him to forge connections with diverse groups of people, even those who had once been his oppressors.

Mandela's journey through life was filled with challenges, and during his 27 years of imprisonment, he found solace in self-reflection. In the solitude of his cell, he contemplated his own emotions, thoughts, and experiences. This introspection allowed him to develop a deep understanding of himself, which he later used to connect with others profoundly.

Throughout his life, Mandela made it a priority to be present in every interaction. He gave his full attention to the person he was with, and in doing so, he made them feel valued and heard. This genuine connection fostered trust and opened the door to honest, meaningful dialogue.

Mandela's keen eye for body language allowed him to understand the emotions of those around him, even when words were left unspoken. He could sense the tension in a room, the sadness behind a smile, or the joy in a person's eyes. This skill enabled him to navigate complex social situations and build stronger relationships.

When faced with conflict, Mandela used his empathy and emotional intelligence to defuse tension and promote understanding. He acknowledged and validated the feelings of others, even when he disagreed with their perspectives. By doing so, he created an environment where people felt safe expressing their thoughts and emotions, paving the way for open communication and resolution.

Mandela's journey was not just about understanding others but also about fostering self-awareness. He continually reflected on his emotions and reactions, enabling him to grow as a person and leader. This self-awareness allowed him to recognize and address his own needs, as well as the needs of those around him.

In his quest to unite a divided nation, Mandela employed perspective-taking to understand the experiences and emotions of others better. He put himself in the shoes of those who had suffered under apartheid and those who had enforced it. By doing so, he could empathize with their fears, hopes, and desires, ultimately finding common ground to build a more inclusive and equitable society.

Mandela's compassionate nature significantly impacted his ability to connect with others. He genuinely cared about the well-being of those around him, and his actions reflected this concern. His kindness and understanding were an example for others to follow, inspiring a nation to unite and work toward a brighter future.

Throughout his life, Mandela sought feedback from friends, family, and colleagues to improve his empathy and emotional intelligence. He was open to constructive criticism and viewed it as an opportunity to grow and evolve as a leader. This willingness to learn and adapt allowed him to continuously hone his skills and become a more effective and compassionate leader.

In conclusion, willpower is the vital force that binds the elements of building and maintaining relationships, enhancing communication and conflict resolution, and practicing empathy and emotional intelligence. It empowers individuals to overcome obstacles, persevere through challenges, and commit to nurturing meaningful connections. By harnessing willpower, we foster open and honest dialogue, resolve disputes constructively, and cultivate our capacity for empathy and emotional intelligence, all of which contribute to deeper, more fulfilling relationships and harmonious coexistence with those around us.

Chapter 12: Willpower and Creativity

12.1 Cultivating Creative Discipline

The journey to creative mastery is paved with countless hours of practice, experimentation, and dedication. In a world that often celebrates overnight successes and raw talent, it is essential to remember the indispensable role of creative discipline in unlocking our full potential. By cultivating a disciplined approach to our creative pursuits, we hone our skills and set the stage for breakthroughs and innovation.

Creative discipline is consistently engaging in our chosen art form or creative endeavor, regardless of external circumstances or fluctuations in motivation. It is the commitment to showing up and doing the work, even when inspiration seems elusive or challenges arise. When we embrace creative discipline, we build resilience and fortitude, fostering a mindset of persistence and determination that serves us well in all aspects of life.

One of the most persuasive arguments for cultivating creative discipline is the undeniable link between consistent practice and skill development. As the adage goes, "Practice makes perfect." Dedicating ourselves to regular exercise improves our skills and increases our likelihood of producing exceptional work. This growth is rewarding and motivates us to continue pushing the boundaries of our creative potential.

Creative discipline helps us break free from the constraints of perfectionism and the fear of failure. Committing to the process and focusing on consistent practice allows us to embrace any creative endeavor's inevitable setbacks and mistakes. This mindset liberates us from the paralyzing grip of self-doubt and empowers us to take risks, explore new ideas, and ultimately unleash our creative potential.

Cultivating creative discipline fosters a sense of purpose and direction in our lives. We are more likely to feel engaged, fulfilled, and connected to our innermost passions when dedicated to a creative pursuit. This sense of purpose can serve as a powerful source of motivation, driving us to overcome obstacles and pursue our dreams with unwavering resolve.

Here are some tips on how to cultivate creative discipline:

1. Set clear goals: Establish specific, measurable, achievable, relevant, and time-bound (SMART) goals for your creative pursuits. This will give you a clear direction and a framework for measuring progress.
2. Create a routine: Develop a consistent schedule for your creative practice, whether daily,

weekly, or otherwise. Stick to this routine as much as possible to build discipline and make creativity a habit.

3. Break tasks into smaller steps: Breaking down larger projects into smaller, manageable tasks can make the creative process less daunting and more achievable. This approach allows you to maintain momentum and experience a sense of accomplishment.
4. Prioritize your creative time: Treat your creative practice as a priority rather than something you do only when you have spare time. Schedule your creative sessions and protect this time from other commitments and distractions.
5. Limit distractions: Identify and minimize distractions during your creative practice, whether turning off your phone, finding a quiet space, or using tools like website blockers to stay focused.
6. Find your optimal creative environment: Experiment with different workspaces, lighting, music, and other environmental factors to discover the conditions that best support your creativity and focus.
7. Practice self-compassion: Acknowledge that setbacks and obstacles are a natural part of the

creative process. Be kind to yourself when things don't go as planned, and use these experiences as opportunities for growth and learning.

8. Seek accountability: Share your creative goals with friends, family, or online communities to create a sense of accountability. This can motivate you to stay disciplined and committed to your practice.
9. Reward yourself: Celebrate milestones and accomplishments along your creative journey. This positive reinforcement can help maintain motivation and encourage continued discipline.
10. Stay curious and open to learning: Embrace a growth mindset and seek new ideas, techniques, and perspectives to fuel your creativity and maintain your passion for your craft.
11. Reflect and adjust: Periodically evaluate your progress and adjust your goals, routine, or approach as needed. This reflection can help you stay on track and ensure your creative discipline aligns with your evolving interests and aspirations.

Stephen King, the renowned author with a career spanning over five decades, embodies creative discipline fueled by willpower. With more than 60 novels and 200 short stories under his belt, King's success is a testament to his dedication to his craft. The following narrative explores King's journey in cultivating creative discipline through his actions and experiences.

King's daily writing routine is a cornerstone of his creative discipline. Without exception, he writes 2,000 words daily, consistently producing high-quality work throughout his career. This unwavering commitment has formed the foundation of his prolific success.

Treating writing as his primary job and the most important aspect of his life, King ensures he carves out space and time for writing each day. By prioritizing his craft above all else, he remains dedicated to his creative pursuits regardless of other commitments or distractions.

King faced numerous personal challenges, including addiction and a near-fatal accident. However, these setbacks did not deter him from writing. Instead, his creative discipline overcame adversity, allowing him to continue producing exceptional work despite hardship.

King firmly believes in embracing the creative process and organically letting the story take shape. By allowing his creativity to flow freely, he can craft more engaging and original stories that captivate readers worldwide.

Another vital aspect of King's creative discipline is his trust in his subconscious mind. By relying on his imagination to guide him, he discovers unexpected twists and turns in his stories, contributing to his unique and captivating narrative style.

When faced with writer's block, King chooses to push through the obstacle by continuing to write. He recognizes that maintaining creative discipline and overcoming barriers are crucial for sustained success and personal growth.

Early in his career, King encountered numerous rejections from publishers. However, he refused to let these setbacks discourage him. Instead, he remained committed to his craft, writing and submitting his work until he found success.

King's commitment to continuous learning and growth as a writer is evident in his avid reading habits. By constantly seeking inspiration and knowledge from other writers, he refines his skills and remains motivated to produce exceptional work.

Throughout his career, King has often worked on multiple projects simultaneously. This approach helps him stay productive, keeps his creativity fresh, and prevents burnout.

King's collaborations with other authors, filmmakers, and artists on various projects allowed him to expand his horizons and learn from other creative minds. These partnerships have enriched his work and contributed to his writing growth.

King adapts to the evolving storytelling landscape by embracing new technologies and mediums, such as digital publishing and social media. This adaptability has enabled him to stay relevant and continue reaching new audiences.

Above all, Stephen King's unwavering commitment to his craft is the driving force behind his creative discipline. His passion for storytelling and dedication to honing his skills have resulted in an illustrious career, earning him a place among the most celebrated authors in history.

12.2 Overcoming Creative Blocks and Procrastination

In creative work, one often encounters obstacles that hinder the flow of ideas and stall progress. Creative blocks and procrastination are common challenges that even the most accomplished artists face. However, through the relentless pursuit of progress and the application of willpower, these barriers can be conquered, paving the way for uninhibited creativity.

Creative blocks manifest as mental roadblocks that inhibit inspiration, preventing artists from accessing their full creative potential. They can arise from various sources, such as self-doubt, fear of failure, or external pressures. One must confront the underlying causes and exercise willpower to push through the mental fog to dismantle these obstructions. By embracing vulnerability and allowing oneself to venture into uncharted territory, the creative spirit is liberated, and new ideas emerge.

Procrastination, another formidable adversary, arises when an individual postpones tasks or delays taking action. This avoidance can stem from various factors, including fear of inadequacy, perfectionism, or the mere preference for immediate gratification. One must summon the willpower to initiate action and maintain momentum to overcome procrastination. By breaking tasks into smaller, manageable steps and focusing on the process rather than the outcome, one can effectively counteract the tendency to delay.

As artists and creatives confront these challenges, they may employ various strategies to bolster their willpower and maintain forward momentum. Setting attainable goals, establishing routines, and creating a conducive work environment can facilitate the cultivation of discipline and focus. Additionally, seeking external support from mentors, peers, or accountability partners can provide valuable encouragement and motivation.

Ultimately, overcoming creative blocks and procrastination requires a steadfast commitment to pursuing progress. With unwavering willpower and the determination to surmount obstacles, creatives can forge ahead, realizing their full potential and achieving their artistic aspirations.

Here are some tips on how to use willpower to overcome creative blocks and procrastination:

1. Embrace imperfection: Allow yourself to create imperfect work initially, knowing you can refine and improve it later. This mindset can reduce the pressure to produce perfect results, making it easier to begin and maintain progress.
2. Set a timer: Use the Pomodoro Technique or a similar time management method to work in focused intervals, with short breaks in between. This can help increase productivity and prevent procrastination.
3. Change your environment: If you are stuck in a creative rut, try working in a new location or altering your surroundings to stimulate fresh ideas and inspiration.
4. Identify your peak productivity times: Determine when you are most alert and

creative during the day, and schedule your work sessions accordingly to maximize your productivity and willpower.

5. Engage in physical activity: Regular exercise can help boost your energy levels, improve your mood, and enhance your cognitive function, all of which contribute to overcoming creative blocks and procrastination.
6. Practice mindfulness: Incorporate mindfulness techniques, such as meditation or deep breathing exercises, to help you stay present and focused on the task.
7. Eliminate decision fatigue: Simplify your daily routine and minimize the number of daily decisions you must make. This can help conserve your mental energy for creative work.
8. Visualize success: Imagine the accomplishment and satisfaction you will experience after completing your creative project. Use this visualization to motivate yourself to push through challenges and stay on track.
9. Seek inspiration: Expose yourself to new ideas and experiences by reading, watching movies, attending events, or conversing with others. This can help reignite your creative spark and

provide fresh perspectives to overcome creative blocks.

10. Set deadlines: Impose self-imposed deadlines to create a sense of urgency and encourage you to focus on completing tasks. Share these deadlines with someone else to increase your sense of accountability.
11. Monitor your progress: Keep track of your accomplishments and setbacks to maintain awareness of your progress and identify areas for improvement. This self-reflection can help you stay motivated and adjust your approach as needed.
12. Cultivate self-compassion: Acknowledge that creative blocks and procrastination are natural challenges many people face. Be kind to yourself when you struggle, and use these experiences as opportunities for growth and learning.

The story of Elizabeth Gilbert, the acclaimed author of "Eat, Pray, Love," is a compelling example of how willpower can help overcome creative blocks and procrastination. Gilbert's journey through personal challenges and her determination to pursue her passion for writing showcase her strength and perseverance in adversity.

Elizabeth Gilbert had always been passionate about writing, even when her work did not immediately garner widespread attention. For years, she worked diligently on her craft, writing in her spare time while juggling various day jobs to support herself. This dedication to her passion demonstrated her willpower to overcome obstacles and prioritize her creative pursuits.

After experiencing a painful divorce and a subsequent period of depression, Gilbert made the brave decision to embark on a year-long journey of self-discovery. Her travels took her to Italy, India, and Indonesia, where she sought healing, spiritual growth, and personal fulfillment. This transformative experience inspired her memoir, "Eat, Pray, Love."

While writing "Eat, Pray, Love," Gilbert faced numerous creative blocks as she struggled to find the right words to convey her experiences and emotions. She relied on her willpower and discipline to overcome these challenges, committing to a daily writing routine and setting attainable goals.

When she felt stuck, Gilbert used visualization techniques to imagine the completion of her book and the sense of accomplishment it would bring. This mental exercise helped motivate her to push through her creative blocks and maintain focus on her project.

To prevent procrastination, Gilbert set deadlines for herself, creating a sense of urgency that encouraged her to stay on track. She shared these deadlines with her editor and friends, increasing her sense of accountability and commitment to completing her work.

When Gilbert struggled with writer's block, she sought inspiration from various sources. She read books, watched movies, and conversed with others to reignite her creative spark and gain fresh perspectives on her experiences.

Gilbert also practiced mindfulness techniques to help her stay present and focused while writing. She cultivated a sense of calm and concentration that facilitated her creative process by incorporating meditation and deep breathing exercises into her daily routine.

Gilbert broke her writing tasks into smaller, manageable steps to maintain her momentum and keep her creativity flowing. Despite challenges and setbacks, this approach allowed her to progress steadily on her book.

To conserve her mental energy for writing, Gilbert simplified her daily routine and minimized the daily decisions she needed to make. This strategy enabled her to dedicate more time and focus to her creative work.

Throughout the writing process, Gilbert tracked her progress and reflected on her accomplishments and setbacks. This self-awareness allowed her to adjust her approach and stay motivated to reach her goals.

Finally, Gilbert cultivated self-compassion, acknowledging that creative blocks and procrastination are natural challenges many artists face. By treating herself with kindness and using her struggles as opportunities for growth, she overcame these obstacles and completed her memoir.

12.3 Nurturing Passion and Curiosity

The quest for creativity, passion, and curiosity serves as vital catalysts, igniting innovation and driving the pursuit of excellence. By nurturing these intrinsic qualities, individuals can harness their willpower to foster a thriving creative life, ultimately transcending the boundaries of their imagination.

Passion, an intense enthusiasm or desire for a particular subject or activity, provides the motivational force that propels individuals toward their creative goals. When harnessed, passion stimulates the determination to persist, even in adversity or setbacks. As individuals nurture their passion, they develop an unwavering commitment to their craft, dedicating themselves wholeheartedly to developing their skills and realizing their creative vision.

Curiosity, the innate desire to explore and understand the world, fuels the creative process by prompting individuals to question, experiment, and seek novel perspectives. Through inquiry, individuals can cultivate an open-mindedness that allows them to embrace ambiguity and complexity, fostering a fertile environment to germinate innovative ideas. By nurturing curiosity, individuals can transform their creative endeavors, opening doors to uncharted territories and expanding the horizons of possibility.

To nurture passion and curiosity, individuals must actively engage in activities that stimulate their interests and challenge their creative boundaries. By immersing themselves in their chosen field, they can deepen their knowledge and expertise, cultivating a richer understanding of their creative landscape. Additionally, individuals can benefit from exposing themselves to diverse sources of inspiration, such as books, films, music, and conversations with others, to broaden their creative palate and spark new ideas.

In pursuing creativity, individuals need to balance their passion and curiosity with a healthy dose of discipline and willpower. By dedicating time and effort to their creative endeavors, they can maintain the momentum necessary to overcome obstacles and achieve their goals. Furthermore, individuals must remain adaptable and receptive to change, as the creative journey often involves unexpected twists and turns that require flexibility and resilience.

Below are some great examples of how passion and curiosity change our world.

The invention of the telephone can be traced back to Alexander Graham Bell's passion for communication and his relentless curiosity about the science of sound. Bell's mother and wife both had hearing impairments, which fueled his desire to find ways for people to communicate more effectively. Through years of experimentation and persistence, Bell's inquisitive nature led to the creation of the telephone, an invention that revolutionized how humans interact and connect.

The Wright brothers', Orville and Wilbur, story demonstrates how their passion for flight and insatiable curiosity led to the development of the first powered, controlled, and sustained airplane. The brothers spent countless hours studying the mechanics of birds in flight, meticulously observing and analyzing their movements. Their relentless pursuit of knowledge and understanding enabled them to overcome numerous obstacles, ultimately resulting in the birth of modern aviation and changing the way humans travel and explore the world.

Marie Curie's passion for science and deep-rooted curiosity drove her to make groundbreaking discoveries in radioactivity. Despite facing numerous challenges as a woman in a male-dominated field, Curie persevered and became the first to win two Nobel Prizes, one in Physics and another in Chemistry. Her discoveries, including the isolation of radium and polonium, revolutionized the field of science and paved the way for advancements in medical treatments and technology.

Thomas Edison's insatiable curiosity and passion for inventing led to the development of the incandescent light bulb, the phonograph, and many other inventions that have shaped the modern world. Edison's relentless experimentation and ability to learn from failure enabled him to achieve significant breakthroughs in various fields, including electricity, communication, and entertainment. His innovations transformed the daily lives of millions of people and continue to influence the world today.

Steve Jobs, the visionary co-founder of Apple Inc., exemplified how passion and curiosity could change the world through technological innovation. Jobs had an innate desire to create functional and aesthetically pleasing products. His unwavering dedication to design and user experience, coupled with his ability to anticipate the needs and desires of consumers, led to the development of revolutionary products such as the Macintosh computer, iPod, iPhone, and iPad. These inventions have had an enormous impact on the way people live, work, and communicate.

Lastly, the story of Jonas Salk demonstrates how passion and curiosity can lead to life-saving innovations. Salk was a medical researcher driven to find a cure for polio, a debilitating disease affecting millions worldwide. His passion for finding a solution and his curiosity about the intricacies of the disease led him to develop the first successful polio vaccine. Salk's groundbreaking work saved countless lives and changed the course of history in public health.

These examples show that when passion and curiosity are nurtured and harnessed, individuals can create groundbreaking innovations that impact the world. Through their relentless pursuit of knowledge and understanding, these individuals were able to transform industries, save lives, and redefine the limits of human potential.

Lewis Terman, a renowned psychologist, began his study in the 1920s with over 1,500 gifted children in California, tracking their development over several decades. Terman's study aimed to investigate the factors that contributed to the success and well-being of these intellectually gifted individuals.

The study evaluated participants for various psychological traits, including curiosity and passion.

Researchers regularly collected data on their academic achievements, professional accomplishments, and personal well-being.

The findings of Terman's study revealed that participants with higher levels of curiosity and passion were likelier to achieve personal and professional success. They were more inclined to engage in lifelong learning, pursue higher education, and excel in their chosen careers. Moreover, these individuals reported higher levels of life satisfaction and overall happiness.

In contrast, participants with average or lower levels of curiosity and passion were found to have a more challenging time attaining personal and professional success. They were less likely to excel academically or professionally and often reported lower life satisfaction and happiness.

Terman's longitudinal study of gifted children provides valuable insights into the importance of curiosity and passion in shaping success and fulfillment in life. It highlights the benefits of nurturing these traits, leading to greater achievements and a more meaningful and satisfied life.

Chapter 13: Willpower in Leadership and Management

13.1 The Power of Self-Control for Effective Leadership

In the realm of leadership, willpower and self-control are pivotal qualities that can make or break one's ability to guide others. These attributes empower leaders to maintain composure in challenging situations, make informed decisions, and inspire confidence in their followers. The power of self-control is a vital element for effective leadership, as it allows individuals to navigate the complexities of human interactions, emotions, and the uncertainties that come with managing people.

Imagine a captain at the helm of a ship, steering it through a stormy sea. The waves crash against the vessel, threatening to capsize it, and the wind roars through the sails, pulling the ship off course. Amidst the chaos, the captain remains calm and composed, holding tight to the wheel and guiding the ship toward safer waters. This image of steadfast resilience under pressure embodies self-control in leadership.

One must delve into its psychological foundations to understand self-control's power. Self-control regulates emotions, thoughts, and behaviors, even when faced with temptation or difficulty. This capacity is essential for leaders, enabling them to focus on long-term goals and resist the allure of short-term gratification. A leader with strong self-control will withstand the pressures of their position, making decisions based on reason and foresight rather than being swayed by fleeting emotions or immediate concerns. As a result, they will be better equipped to handle the various challenges that come their way, from managing tight deadlines to navigating interpersonal conflicts within their team.

Furthermore, self-control in leadership directly impacts the development of trust and credibility. When leaders exhibit self-discipline and restraint, they demonstrate to their followers that they can be relied upon to make rational decisions, even under duress. This fosters a sense of security and trust within the team, as members can confidently believe in their leader's ability to steer them in the right direction. This trust is a solid foundation for a healthy, productive working environment where employees feel inspired and motivated to contribute their best efforts.

In addition to fostering trust, self-control is vital in conflict resolution and decision-making. Leaders with strong self-control are more capable of approaching challenging situations with a level-headed, objective mindset, thereby minimizing the influence of personal biases or emotions. This allows them to assess the situation accurately, weigh the available options, and choose the most appropriate course of action. By doing so, they can avoid impulsive decisions that may lead to undesirable consequences for the team and the organization.

In 2010, a seminal research paper by psychologists Wilhelm Hofmann, Roy F. Baumeister, Georg Förster, and Kathleen D. Vohs provided compelling evidence supporting the idea that self-control plays a critical role in effective leadership. The paper "Everyday Temptations: An Experience Sampling Study of Desire, Conflict, and Self-Control" presented an innovative approach to measuring self-control and its impact on individuals' daily lives, including decision-making and goal attainment.

The researchers employed the experience sampling method, which involved participants recording their desires, conflicts, and instances of self-control throughout the day. Over a week, 205 participants provided data on their everyday experiences, enabling the researchers to analyze the relationship between self-control, goal pursuit, and leadership-relevant outcomes.

One of the study's key findings was that individuals with higher self-control exhibited tremendous success in achieving their goals, particularly in the face of conflicting desires. This result underscored the importance of self-control in enabling people to focus on their long-term objectives, even when confronted with short-term temptations or challenges.

Another significant finding was that individuals with higher self-control experienced fewer conflicts between their desires and goals. This suggests that self-control not only helps leaders resist distractions but also allows them to structure their lives to minimize potential conflicts. By doing so, they can create an environment more conducive to effective decision-making and goal attainment.

In addition to these insights, the study revealed that practice could enhance self-control. This is particularly relevant to leadership, as it implies that individuals can develop and strengthen their self-control over time, improving their effectiveness as leaders. By engaging in self-control exercises and adopting habits that promote self-regulation, aspiring leaders can cultivate the discipline required to navigate the challenges and complexities of their roles.

Furthermore, the research demonstrated that self-control is critical not only for leaders themselves but also for their followers. Individuals with higher self-control were more effective in supporting and guiding their peers, as they were better equipped to manage interpersonal conflicts and focus on shared objectives. This finding underscores the importance of self-control in fostering a collaborative and harmonious team dynamic, which is crucial for overall organizational success.

The study also highlighted the potential consequences of depleted self-control resources, such as increased vulnerability to impulsive decision-making and reduced ability to manage stress. Leaders who experience diminished self-control may find it challenging to resist distractions or make objective, well-informed decisions, potentially leading to suboptimal outcomes for their team or organization.

In light of these findings, the paper offers valuable recommendations for organizations seeking to develop influential leaders. By prioritizing self-control as a key leadership competency, organizations can ensure that their leaders possess the skills and qualities necessary to navigate the demands of their roles successfully. This may involve providing training programs and resources designed to enhance self-control or implementing strategies to mitigate the risk of ego depletion.

Moreover, the study's results affect the broader management and organizational behavior field. Researchers and practitioners can develop more targeted interventions and strategies to optimize leader performance by understanding self-control's vital role in effective leadership. This may include designing organizational structures and policies that support self-control, such as promoting work-life balance, encouraging regular breaks, and facilitating open communication among team members.

Howard Schultz grew up in a low-income housing project in Brooklyn, New York. He experienced firsthand the challenges of living in poverty, which fueled his desire to create a better life for himself and his family. Despite these hardships, Schultz remained focused on his goals, exhibiting high self-control from a young age.

Schultz's passion for sports helped him secure an athletic scholarship to Northern Michigan University. He demonstrated remarkable discipline and determination to succeed academically as a student, eventually graduating with a bachelor's degree in business administration.

After graduation, Schultz pursued a career in sales and marketing. In 1981, he joined Starbucks, a small coffee shop chain based in Seattle. Schultz quickly recognized the company's potential but saw an opportunity to transform the business into something more significant.

During a trip to Italy, Schultz was captivated by the vibrant coffee culture and community surrounding the local espresso bars. He believed that this unique experience could be replicated in the United States and that Starbucks could become a "third place" between home and work where people could connect and build relationships.

However, Schultz faced resistance from the original owners, who were hesitant to deviate from their initial vision for Starbucks. Undeterred by this setback, Schultz demonstrated exceptional self-control and resilience by leaving the company to start his coffee shop, Il Giornale.

Il Giornale quickly gained popularity, and in 1987, Schultz purchased Starbucks and merged the two companies. As the new CEO, he set out to expand Starbucks nationwide, focusing on creating a welcoming and comfortable environment in each store.

During this period of growth, Schultz faced numerous challenges, including intense competition, economic

downturns, and the need to adapt to ever-changing consumer preferences. His unwavering self-control and strategic thinking allowed him to navigate these obstacles effectively and make informed decisions that positioned Starbucks for long-term success.

One of the most notable examples of Schultz's self-control in leadership was his decision to close all Starbucks stores in the United States for a day in 2008 to retrain employees and refocus on the quality of their coffee. This bold move demonstrated his commitment to upholding the brand's standards, even when facing financial pressures and public scrutiny.

Throughout his CEO tenure, Schultz also showed a strong commitment to social responsibility and ethical business practices. He prioritized employee welfare, offering comprehensive benefits packages and creating a supportive work environment. Schultz's self-control and focus on long-term goals allowed him to make decisions that not only benefited the company but also had a positive impact on society.

In 2012, Schultz stepped down as CEO but continued to serve as Starbucks' Executive Chairman. He used this position to advocate for critical social issues, such as addressing income inequality and supporting veterans. His self-control enabled him to effectively leverage his influence and inspire change within and outside the company.

Schultz's leadership journey is a testament to the power of self-control in achieving success. From his humble beginnings to his rise as a prominent business leader, Schultz consistently demonstrated the ability to resist short-term temptations and remain focused on his long-term vision.

13.2 Decision-Making and Problem-Solving under Pressure

Leadership is often defined by the ability to make sound decisions and solve complex problems, especially when the stakes are high and time is of the essence. Maintaining composure and thinking critically under pressure is crucial in this fast-paced and demanding environment. This section will persuasively argue the importance of effective decision-making and problem-solving skills in challenging situations and explore the role of self-control in fostering these abilities.

First, let us consider the impact of high-pressure situations on the decision-making process. When confronted with stress, our cognitive resources become strained, increasing the likelihood of succumbing to cognitive biases and making impulsive choices. As a result, leaders must develop the ability to stay composed and rational even in the face of adversity, enabling them to make more informed and strategic decisions that benefit their team and organization.

In high-stress scenarios, problem-solving skills are equally important. Leaders who can quickly analyze a situation, identify potential solutions, and implement the most effective course of action are invaluable assets to any organization. Leaders must possess technical expertise, vital emotional intelligence, and self-control to excel in this domain. These qualities allow them to navigate the complexities of human dynamics and adapt their approach as needed.

One essential aspect of decision-making and problem-solving under pressure is the ability to prioritize. In high-stakes situations, leaders must be able to distinguish between urgent and essential tasks, allocating their time and resources accordingly. This requires high self-control, as it involves resisting the temptation to focus on short-term gains or simple tasks that may provide immediate gratification but ultimately detract from long-term goals.

Another key element of effective decision-making and problem-solving is being objective and open-minded. Under pressure, it takes a lot of work to avoid relying on preconceived notions or assumptions, limiting a leader's ability to identify innovative solutions or recognize emerging opportunities. By exercising self-control and maintaining a balanced perspective, leaders can avoid these pitfalls and foster a more creative, adaptive approach to problem-solving.

Communication is also critical in high-pressure decision-making and problem-solving scenarios. Leaders must clearly and effectively convey their expectations, goals, and rationale to their team, ensuring everyone is aligned and working toward a common objective. This requires a high degree of self-control, as leaders must resist the urge to micromanage or dictate every aspect of the process, instead fostering an environment of trust and collaboration.

In the high-stakes world of leadership, the ability to make sound decisions and solve problems under pressure can often mean the difference between success and failure. One real-world leader who exemplifies this ability is Chesley "Sully" Sullenberger, the retired airline captain who successfully landed US Airways Flight 1549 on the Hudson River in 2009, saving the lives of all 155 passengers and crew members on board.

On January 15, 2009, Captain Sullenberger faced an extraordinary crisis when, shortly after takeoff from LaGuardia Airport in New York City, his Airbus A320 struck a flock of geese, resulting in the loss of both engines. With only minutes to assess the situation and determine the best course of action, Sullenberger demonstrated remarkable poise and decision-making skills under immense pressure.

As the aircraft rapidly lost altitude, Sullenberger and his co-pilot, Jeffrey Skiles, considered various options, including attempting to return to LaGuardia or diverting to Teterboro Airport in New Jersey. However, Sullenberger quickly realized neither airport was viable, given the plane's rapidly decreasing altitude and speed. In a split-second decision, he determined that everyone on board's best chance of survival was to attempt a water landing on the Hudson River.

This decision required a clear understanding of the aircraft's capabilities and a calm and focused mindset to execute the high-risk maneuver. As the plane descended toward the river, Sullenberger maintained a steady hand on the controls, expertly adjusting the aircraft's speed and angle to ensure the safest possible landing.

As the Airbus A320 touched down on the frigid waters of the Hudson River, passengers and crew members braced for impact, unsure of the outcome. Miraculously, the plane remained intact upon landing, allowing everyone on board to evacuate onto the wings and into the inflatable life rafts. Sullenberger's quick thinking and decisive action under pressure saved the lives of everyone on the plane, earning him widespread praise and admiration.

In the aftermath of the incident, the media, aviation experts, and political leaders lauded Captain Sullenberger's extraordinary feat. His calm demeanor and ability to make critical decisions under extreme pressure were cited as key factors in the successful outcome of the harrowing event. The incident soon became known as the "Miracle on the Hudson," and Sullenberger emerged as a national hero.

Beyond his actions in the cockpit, Sullenberger also demonstrated exceptional leadership in the moments following the water landing. After ensuring that all passengers and crew members had evacuated the aircraft, he made two additional sweeps through the cabin to verify that no one had been left behind. This selfless courage further underscored his commitment to the well-being of those under his care.

In the years since the "Miracle on the Hudson," Sullenberger has used his newfound platform to advocate for improved aviation safety and training standards. Drawing on his experiences as a pilot and his expertise in decision-making under pressure, he has contributed valuable insights to the ongoing discussion surrounding aviation safety and human factors.

Sullenberger's story is a powerful reminder of the importance of decision-making and problem-solving under pressure in leadership. His ability to assess a dire situation quickly, weigh the available options, and make a courageous decision despite overwhelming odds offers a compelling example for leaders in all fields.

13.3 Leading by Example: Inspiring and Motivating Others

The power of leading by example as a way to inspire and motivate others has long been recognized as a crucial aspect of effective leadership. A study conducted by Harvard Business School, titled "The Contaminating Effects of Building Instrumental Ties: How Networking Can Make Us Feel Dirty" by Tiziana Casciaro, Francesca Gino, and Maryam Kouchaki, offers valuable insights into the importance of willpower and authenticity in leading by example.

The study examined the psychological effects of networking on individuals and discovered that those who approached networking with a genuine desire to help others and build meaningful relationships experienced more positive emotions and feelings of self-worth. Conversely, networking solely for personal gain often felt inauthentic and "dirty," negatively impacting their motivation and job satisfaction.

This research highlights the importance of willpower and self-control in leading by example. Leaders who demonstrate genuine concern for the well-being of their team members, colleagues, and organization are more likely to inspire and motivate those around them. By exercising self-control and consistently prioritizing the needs of others over their self-interest, leaders can foster a positive, supportive work environment that encourages collaboration, innovation, and growth.

Moreover, the study also revealed that individuals who approached networking with a genuine desire to help others were more likely to establish meaningful connections and build trust with their peers. This finding underscores the importance of willpower in developing strong, authentic relationships that can enhance teamwork, communication, and overall organizational performance.

By leading with integrity and consistently demonstrating a commitment to the well-being of others, leaders can also cultivate a culture of accountability and high performance within their organizations. Employees who always observe their leaders making decisions based on the team's and the company's best interests are more likely to feel motivated to uphold these same values and standards. This sense of shared purpose and collective responsibility can foster a strong camaraderie and dedication among team members, ultimately driving improved performance and results.

In addition to fostering a positive work culture, leading by example through willpower and self-control can enhance a leader's credibility and influence. When leaders consistently demonstrate their ability to resist short-term temptations and prioritize long-term goals, they signal their followers that they possess the discipline, foresight, and self-awareness necessary to navigate complex challenges and make sound decisions. This can enhance their authority and inspire trust and confidence in their followers, making it easier for them to rally support for their initiatives and drive change within the organization.

Furthermore, leaders who consistently demonstrate willpower and self-control are more likely to be perceived as authentic and genuine by their followers. This authenticity can be a powerful tool for inspiring loyalty, commitment, and engagement among team members, who may be more willing to go the extra mile for a leader they perceive to be honest, transparent, and true to their values.

The Harvard Business School study also offers valuable insights for organizations seeking to develop and nurture influential leaders. By prioritizing willpower and self-control as key leadership competencies, organizations can ensure that their leaders have the skills and mindset necessary to inspire and motivate their teams. This may include providing training and development opportunities focusing on building self-awareness, emotional intelligence, and resilience and implementing policies and practices encouraging ethical behavior and decision-making.

Moreover, organizations can also benefit from promoting a culture that values and rewards leading by example. By recognizing and celebrating leaders who demonstrate willpower, self-control, and a genuine commitment to the well-being of their teams and the organization, companies can reinforce the importance of these traits and encourage others to follow suit.

In today's fast-paced, ever-evolving business landscape, inspiring and motivating others is a critical skill for leaders at all levels. By cultivating willpower and self-control and consistently demonstrating these qualities in their actions, leaders can set a powerful example for their followers and foster a positive, high-performing work environment that drives success.

Sir Ernest Shackleton was a British explorer who led several expeditions to the Antarctic during the early 20th century. His incredible story of leadership, determination, and perseverance serves as a powerful illustration of the importance of leading by example.

Shackleton is best known for his 1914-1916 Imperial Trans-Antarctic Expedition, also known as the Endurance Expedition. The goal of this expedition was to traverse the Antarctic continent. Still, it quickly turned into a harrowing test of survival and leadership when the expedition ship, the Endurance, became trapped in pack ice.

As the ice slowly crushed the ship, Shackleton and his crew of 27 men faced an incredibly challenging situation. Stranded in one of the most inhospitable environments on Earth, they were forced to abandon their original mission and focus on the seemingly impossible task of returning home alive.

Throughout the ordeal, Shackleton demonstrated exceptional leadership by consistently putting the well-being of his crew first. He ensured that every team member had equal access to food and other resources, often sacrificing his comfort to ensure the survival of others. His selfless actions and unwavering commitment to his crew were powerful examples that motivated the team to persevere through difficult circumstances.

Shackleton also displayed remarkable resourcefulness and adaptability in the face of adversity. When the ice finally crushed the Endurance, he led his crew across the treacherous ice floes to the relative safety of Elephant Island. Recognizing that rescue was unlikely to come to them. He boldly decided to set out on a daring 800-mile open-boat journey across the treacherous Southern Ocean to seek help. With only five other crew members, Shackleton navigated the tiny lifeboat, the James Caird, through one of the world's most dangerous stretches of water, enduring freezing temperatures, monstrous waves, and constant exhaustion.

Upon reaching South Georgia Island, Shackleton and two crew members embarked on an arduous 36-hour trek across the island's mountainous terrain to reach a remote whaling station. Despite facing seemingly insurmountable odds, Shackleton's determination and willpower never wavered, and he eventually secured the help needed to rescue the remaining crew members stranded on Elephant Island.

Throughout the ordeal, Shackleton's unwavering dedication to his crew and ability to lead by example inspired and motivated his men. Not a single member of the expedition was lost, a testament to the resilience and unity of the group under Shackleton's extraordinary leadership.

Shackleton's story demonstrates the power of leading by example, even in extreme and challenging circumstances. His actions showed that a leader's commitment to the well-being and success of their team could inspire and motivate others to overcome adversity and achieve the impossible.

In addition to his incredible feats of physical endurance and determination, Shackleton's leadership was also marked by his ability to foster camaraderie and unity among his crew. He understood the importance of maintaining morale and consciously engaged with his men, sharing their struggles and celebrating their successes. This genuine connection and concern for his team members further reinforced their loyalty and commitment to the mission, despite seemingly insurmountable challenges. Shackleton's leadership style also exemplified the importance of adaptability and flexibility in changing circumstances. When the original mission became impossible, he quickly pivoted and refocused his team's efforts on the new goal of survival and rescue. This ability to adapt and adjust to unforeseen challenges is a critical aspect of effective leadership, and Shackleton's example serves as a powerful reminder of its importance.

Furthermore, Shackleton's story highlights the significance of perseverance and resilience in leadership. Despite facing numerous setbacks and seemingly hopeless situations, he remained steadfast in his determination to bring his entire crew home safely. His unwavering resolve and commitment to his team inspired them to keep going, even when all hope seemed lost. Sir Ernest Shackleton's incredible story of survival and leadership in the Antarctic serves as a potent example of the power of leading by example to inspire and motivate others. Shackleton left an indelible mark on the annals of history and leadership by consistently prioritizing the well-being of his crew, displaying remarkable adaptability in the face of adversity, and demonstrating unwavering perseverance and resilience.

Chapter 14: Willpower and Physical Health

14.1 Building Discipline for Exercise and Fitness

"Strength does not come from physical capacity. It comes from an indomitable will."

- Mahatma Gandhi.

Strong willpower can be the foundation for a healthy lifestyle, driving you to prioritize exercise and fitness in your daily routine. In this section, we will explore the importance of building discipline for exercise and fitness and provide expert insights to guide you on your journey to physical health.

As fitness expert Jillian Michaels once said, "It's not about perfect. It's about effort. And when you bring that effort every single day, that's where transformation happens. That's how change occurs."

Building discipline for exercise and fitness is about consistent effort and perseverance.

To develop discipline for exercise and fitness, follow these expert recommendations:

1. Set realistic goals: Establishing attainable fitness goals is critical to maintaining motivation. As renowned personal trainer Tony Horton advises, "Do your best and forget the rest." Focus on progress, not perfection.

2. Create a routine: Consistency is key to building discipline. By incorporating exercise into your daily schedule, it becomes a habit. Fitness coach and author Chalene Johnson emphasizes, "The secret to success is found in your daily routine."

3. Find an exercise you enjoy: If you want the activity, you will likely stay committed. As fitness expert Chris Freytag explains, "Exercise should be like a celebration of what your body can do, not a punishment for what you ate."

4. Surround yourself with supportive individuals: Seek out friends, family members, or workout partners who share your fitness goals and can help keep you accountable. As a social psychologist, Dr. David McClelland, suggests, "We become the average of the five people we spend the most time with."

5. Be patient and stay committed: Building discipline takes time and dedication. As author and motivational speaker Jim Rohn reminds us, "Success is nothing more than a few simple disciplines practiced every day."

6. Learn from setbacks: Experiencing setbacks is a natural part of any fitness journey. Instead of becoming discouraged, use these moments as

opportunities to learn and grow. As former professional football player Jerry Rice states, "Today I will do what others won't, so tomorrow I can do what others can't."

By implementing these strategies, you can strengthen your willpower and build the discipline necessary for a lifetime of exercise and fitness.

As author and entrepreneur James Clear assert, "You do not rise to the level of your goals. You fall to the level of your systems." Create a strong foundation of discipline and willpower, and you'll be well on your way to achieving your fitness goals.

Eric O'Grey, a 50-year-old man from San Jose, California, was once morbidly obese, weighing over 300 pounds. He struggled with various health issues, such as high blood pressure, type 2 diabetes, and high cholesterol. His doctor warned him that he would have only a few years to live if he didn't change his lifestyle significantly.

One day, while watching a television show about the benefits of a plant-based diet, Eric became inspired to take control of his life. He consulted a nutritionist, who recommended a whole-food, plant-based diet and regular exercise. Eric also adopted a rescue dog named Peety, who became his walking and running companion.

The transformation began slowly but steadily. Eric started walking for 30 minutes daily with Peety, gradually increasing the duration and intensity of their walks. Eventually, they began jogging together, and Eric's weight dropped dramatically.

As Eric's fitness level improved, he started participating in local 5K races. He continued to push himself, eventually running half marathons and marathons. He even completed several triathlons, showcasing his newfound physical abilities and determination.

Eric's unwavering willpower and dedication to his health and fitness paid off. In just over two years, he lost over 150 pounds and reversed his type 2 diabetes, high blood pressure, and high cholesterol. His story has been featured on numerous news outlets, such as CNN and the Today Show, inspiring others with his incredible journey.

The bond between Eric and Peety played a crucial role in his transformation. Peety provided companionship and motivation, helping Eric remain committed to his exercise routine. When Peety passed away, Eric adopted another rescue dog, Jake, who continued to support him on his fitness journey.

Eric's story has since been featured in a documentary called "Eric & Peety," which aims to inspire others struggling with obesity and related health issues. He also wrote a book titled "Walking with Peety: The Dog Who Saved My Life," detailing his life-changing journey.

Today, Eric O'Grey maintains a healthy lifestyle through exercise and a plant-based diet. He actively advocates for the benefits of adopting rescue dogs and the power of self-discipline and strong willpower in achieving personal health and fitness goals.

Eric's story is a testament to the incredible impact of self-discipline and determination on one's health and well-being. Through consistent effort, commitment, and the support of a loyal companion, he was able to turn his life around and inspire countless others to do the same.

Drew Manning, a fit and healthy personal trainer from Utah, realized that he couldn't fully understand his overweight clients' challenges in their weight loss journeys. To gain firsthand experience, he decided to embark on a unique and ambitious experiment: he would gain a significant amount of weight and then lose it, all within a year.

In May 2011, Drew began his "Fit2Fat2Fit" journey. Over six months, he gained 75 pounds by eating an unhealthy diet and abstaining from exercise. His weight ballooned to 269 pounds, and he experienced various health issues, such as sleep apnea, high blood pressure, and low energy levels.

In November 2011, Drew started the second phase of his experiment, aiming to lose the weight he had gained and return to his original fit and healthy state. He shared his journey on his blog, Fit2Fat2Fit.com, and social media platforms, inspiring thousands worldwide to follow his progress.

Drew's weight loss journey was challenging, but he demonstrated unwavering self-discipline and determination. He adopted a healthy diet, focusing on whole foods and portion control, and began a strict exercise routine, which included cardio workouts, weightlifting, and high-intensity interval training (HIIT).

As the weeks passed, Drew's health and fitness levels improved dramatically. He continued documenting his journey, offering advice and encouragement to those inspired by his story. His unique perspective as someone who had experienced both ends of the fitness spectrum resonated with many people struggling with their weight loss journeys.

By June 2012, Drew had successfully lost the 75 pounds he had gained and returned to his original fit state. His story attracted significant media attention, with appearances on Good Morning America, The Tonight Show with Jay Leno, and Dr. Oz, among others.

Since completing his Fit2Fat2Fit journey, Drew has continued to share his experiences and knowledge, authoring a book titled "Fit2Fat2Fit: The Unexpected Lessons from Gaining and Losing 75 lbs. on Purpose" and hosting a popular podcast. He has also developed a successful online fitness program, helping countless people achieve their health and fitness goals.

14.2 Overcoming Barriers to Healthy Eating

"Let food be thy medicine and medicine be thy food."

– Hippocrates

A balanced and nutritious diet is essential to maintaining good health and well-being. However, overcoming barriers to healthy eating can be challenging, especially given the abundance of unhealthy food options and the hectic pace of modern life. This section will explore strategies for overcoming these barriers and provide expert advice to guide you toward a healthier lifestyle.

1. Plan your meals: Meal planning can help you make healthier food choices and prevent impulsive decisions. Registered dietitian and nutritionist Dawn Jackson Blatner advises, "Planning your meals in advance can help you make more nutritious choices, save time, and reduce food waste."

2. Cook at home: Preparing your meals at home allows you to control the ingredients and portion sizes. As celebrity chef Jamie Oliver suggests, "By cooking at home, you can create nutritious and delicious meals using quality ingredients, while also controlling portion sizes and avoiding unhealthy additives."

3. Make healthier substitutions: Swap out unhealthy ingredients for more nutritious alternatives. Nutrition expert and author Michael Pollan advise, "Eat real food. Not too much. Mostly plants." You can improve your overall nutrition by incorporating more fruits, vegetables, whole grains, and lean proteins into your diet.

4. Practice mindful eating: Pay attention to your hunger cues and slowly savor each bite. As mindfulness expert and author Jon Kabat-Zinn recommends, "When you eat, just eat. Engage all your senses in the process, and truly savor the experience."

5. Limit processed and sugary foods: Avoid foods high in sugar, unhealthy fats, and artificial additives. As nutrition researcher and author Dr. Robert Lustig warns, "Sugar is toxic and addictive, leading to numerous health problems." Prioritize whole, unprocessed foods for a healthier diet.

6. Stay hydrated: Drinking water is essential for overall health and can help control hunger and cravings. As a nutrition expert and author, Dr. Fereydoon Batmanghelidj asserts, "You're not sick; you're thirsty. Don't treat thirst with medication."

7. Surround yourself with a supportive network: Connect with friends, family, or online communities who share your healthy eating goals. As psychologist and author Dr. Kelly McGonigal note, "Social support is one of the most powerful predictors of sticking with a new habit or goal."

8. Educate yourself on nutrition: Understanding the basics of nutrition can help you make informed decisions about your diet. As a registered dietitian and nutritionist Ellie Krieger recommends, "Empower yourself with knowledge about nutrition, so you can make healthier choices and feel confident in your decisions."

9. Be patient and forgiving: Adopting a healthier diet takes time and effort. Don't expect perfection; be gentle with yourself when you make mistakes. As author and motivational speaker Brene Brown reminds us, "Imperfections are not inadequacies; they are reminders that we're all in this together."

10. Seek professional guidance if needed: If you're struggling to overcome barriers to healthy eating, consider consulting a registered dietitian or

nutritionist for personalized advice and support. As a renowned nutrition expert and author T. Colin Campbell, advises, "Good nutrition creates health in all areas of our existence."

By implementing these strategies and heeding expert advice, you can overcome barriers to healthy eating and pave the way for a healthier, more vibrant life. Author and motivational speaker Zig Ziglar once said, "You are what you are and where you are because of what has gone into your mind. You change what you are and you change where you are by changing what goes into your mind."

In 2015, the story of Pasquale "Pat" Brocco, a 31-year-old man from Arizona, made headlines for his remarkable transformation. Pat, who once weighed 605 pounds, struggled with numerous health issues, including high blood pressure, high cholesterol, and a high risk of developing diabetes. His doctor warned him that he would face dire consequences if he didn't change his eating habits and lifestyle.

Feeling shocked and determined to turn his life around, Pat took control of his health and overcame the barriers to healthy eating. He began by photographing himself in front of the mirror, using it as motivation and a reminder of where he started.

To jumpstart his weight loss journey, Pat set a personal rule: every time he wanted to eat, he would walk to the nearest Walmart, a mile away from his home. By doing this, he ensured that he walked at least three miles daily. This simple yet effective exercise routine soon evolved into a six-mile daily walk.

As Pat's fitness level increased, so did his determination to improve his diet. He started researching healthy eating habits and making significant changes to his lifestyle. He replaced processed foods and sugary drinks with whole, unprocessed foods such as fruits, vegetables, lean proteins, and whole grains.

Pat also turned to social media to document and share his journey, which helped to hold him accountable and motivated him to stay on track. He used platforms like Instagram and Facebook to connect with others on similar trips, creating a supportive community crucial to his success.

Pat shed an astounding 330 pounds through self-discipline and willpower in just two years. His blood pressure, cholesterol levels, and risk of diabetes all dropped to healthy levels, and he no longer needed the medications he had previously relied on.

Pat took his fitness journey even further with his newfound health and confidence. He began incorporating strength training and bodybuilding exercises into his routine, eventually becoming a personal trainer and motivational speaker to help others overcome their barriers to healthy eating and weight loss.

Pat's incredible story caught the attention of several news outlets, including CNN, Good Morning America, and Inside Edition. Through these platforms, his story reached millions, inspiring countless individuals to take control of their health and well-being.

Pat's journey to better health was not without its challenges. He faced setbacks, plateaus, and moments of doubt but remained steadfast in his commitment to self-discipline and willpower. He continued to push through these obstacles, using his progress and the support of his online community to keep him going. In his own words, Pat has said, "If you want to do something, you can do it. You just have to believe in yourself and take small steps every day." His story is a testament to the power of willpower and self-discipline in achieving one's health and wellness goals.

14.3 Managing Chronic Illness and Pain with Willpower

"Although the world is full of suffering, it is also full of the overcoming of it."

– Helen Keller

Living with chronic illness and pain can be an immense challenge, affecting every aspect of one's life. However, harnessing the power of willpower and self-discipline can help manage the symptoms and improve the overall quality of life. This section will explore strategies for managing chronic illness and pain using willpower, supported by expert advice and quotes.

1. Acceptance and self-compassion: Accepting your situation and practicing self-compassion is crucial in managing chronic illness and pain. Dr. Kristin Neff, a leading expert in self-compassion, states, "When we are in pain, the most important thing we need is not self-improvement; it is self-compassion."

2. Develop a pain management plan: Collaborate with your healthcare team to create a comprehensive plan tailored to your needs. As a pain psychologist, Dr. Judith Scheman advises, "Developing a plan to manage chronic pain is essential to regaining control of your life."

3. Prioritize self-care: Prioritize self-care activities such as sleep, relaxation, and gentle exercise. According to Dr. Gabor Maté, an expert in mind-body medicine, "The essence of healing is self-care and self-awareness."

4. Set realistic goals: Break down larger goals into smaller, achievable steps. Dr. James Fricton, a pain specialist, emphasizes the importance of goal setting, saying, "Setting realistic goals is key to managing chronic pain and living a fulfilling life."

5. Stay connected: Maintain social connections and seek support from friends, family, and support groups. Dr. Brene Brown, a renowned vulnerability and shame researcher, reminds us, "Connection is why we're here; it's what gives purpose and meaning to our lives."

6. Embrace the power of positive thinking: Cultivate an optimistic outlook and focus on the positives, even during challenging times. As Dr. Martin Seligman, the father of positive psychology, says, "Optimism is invaluable for a meaningful life."

7. Practice stress management techniques: Incorporate stress-reducing techniques such as deep breathing exercises, mindfulness, and meditation into your daily routine. Mindfulness expert Jon Kabat-Zinn advises, "You can't stop the waves, but you can learn to surf."

8. Stay informed: Educate yourself about your chronic illness and pain, and stay updated on the latest treatments and research. Knowledge is power, and as Dr. Andrew Weil, an integrative medicine

expert, says, "The more you know, the better choices you can make regarding your health."

9. Prioritize proper nutrition: Adopt a balanced, nutrient-dense diet to support overall health and well-being. As Dr. Mark Hyman, a leading expert in functional medicine, asserts, "The single most powerful tool to reverse your disease and create optimal health is your fork."

10. Be persistent and patient: Managing chronic illness and pain requires persistence and patience. Remember the words of motivational speaker Les Brown: "You don't have to be great to get started, but you have to get started to be great."

By implementing these strategies and heeding the advice of industry experts, you can harness the power of willpower and self-discipline to manage chronic illness and pain more effectively. Embracing a proactive, empowered approach to your health and well-being can lead to a more fulfilling life, even in adversity.

The story of Amy Purdy, a Paralympic snowboarder and motivational speaker, is a powerful example of someone who has used strong willpower to manage chronic illness and pain. Her journey has been well-documented in the media, and her indomitable spirit inspires many.

At 19, Amy was diagnosed with bacterial meningitis, a life-threatening illness that led to amputate her legs below the knees. She also lost both her kidneys and her spleen. Amy's life was turned upside down, and she faced immense physical and emotional pain as she adjusted to her new reality.

However, Amy was determined not to let her circumstances define her. She began the long and arduous rehabilitation process with unwavering willpower and determination. She learned to walk again using prosthetic legs and, despite the chronic pain she experienced, pushed herself to regain her strength and independence.

Amy's journey was not without setbacks. She faced numerous challenges and frustrations as she adapted to her prosthetics and grappled with the limitations of her new body. But through it all, she remained steadfast in her resolve to overcome the obstacles in her path.

One of Amy's passions before her illness was snowboarding. Unwilling to give up on the sport she loved, she set her sights on becoming a professional snowboarder. She worked tirelessly to develop specialized prosthetics that would allow her to snowboard again, and through sheer determination, she returned to the slopes just months after her amputations.

In 2011, Amy co-founded Adaptive Action Sports, a non-profit organization that introduced individuals with physical disabilities to action sports. Her efforts played a significant role in including snowboarding in the 2014 Paralympic Winter Games.

Amy's incredible comeback story caught the media's attention, and she was invited to compete on the 18th season of the popular TV show "Dancing with the Stars." She amazed audiences with her grace and skill, eventually finishing as the runner-up and becoming a fan favorite.

Amy has used her experiences throughout her journey to inspire and empower others facing similar challenges. She has given numerous motivational speeches, sharing her story and the lessons she has learned about resilience, determination, and the power of willpower in overcoming adversity.

In 2018, Amy faced another challenge when she was diagnosed with a severe kidney infection. The infection resulted in losing her transplanted kidney, forcing her to undergo dialysis and wait for a second transplant. Once again, Amy's indomitable willpower shone through as she confronted this new obstacle head-on.

Amy focused on her athletic career despite the physical and emotional toll of her health issues. In 2018, she competed in the Paralympic Winter Games in Pyeongchang, South Korea, earning a silver medal in snowboard cross and a bronze medal in banked slalom.

Amy Purdy's story is a testament to the power of willpower and determination in managing chronic illness and pain. Her resilience in adversity is a potent reminder that we can shape our destiny regardless of life's challenges.

Chapter 15: Willpower and Mental Health

15.1 Developing Mental Resilience

"Life doesn't get easier or more forgiving; we get stronger and more resilient."

– Steve Maraboli

Mental resilience is essential for overcoming life's challenges and maintaining overall mental health. This section will discuss unique strategies for fostering mental resilience, supported by expert advice and quotes.

1. Embrace vulnerability: Acknowledge and express your emotions instead of suppressing them. Dr. Brene Brown, a renowned vulnerability researcher, suggests, "Vulnerability is not a weakness, but rather our most accurate measure of courage."

2. Cultivate curiosity: Approach challenges with curiosity and a desire to learn from them. Psychologist Dr. Todd Kashdan emphasizes, "Curiosity is the engine of growth, and it drives our desire to learn and expand our horizons."

3. Create a sense of purpose: Develop a clear understanding of the purpose that aligns with your values and passions. As Dr. Viktor Frankl states, "Those who have a 'why' to live can bear with almost any 'how.'"

4. Practice mindfulness: Develop mindfulness skills to help you stay present and focused during difficult times. Dr. Jon Kabat-Zinn, a mindfulness expert, advises, "Mindfulness means paying attention in a particular way: on purpose, in the present moment, and nonjudgmentally."

5. Develop emotional intelligence: Improve your ability to recognize, understand, and manage your emotions and those of others. Dr. Daniel Goleman, an expert in emotional intelligence, asserts, "Emotional intelligence is the key to both personal and professional success."

6. Create a support network: Cultivate a diverse network of supportive relationships, including mentors, peers, and friends. As author and motivational speaker Jim Rohn says, "You are the average of the five people you spend the most time with."

7. Prioritize self-care: Ensure you care for your physical, emotional, and mental well-being. Dr. Gabor Maté, an expert in mind-body medicine, emphasizes, "The essence of healing is self-care and self-awareness."

8. Develop a sense of humor: Learn to laugh at yourself and find humor in difficult situations. Comedian Victor Borge once said, "Laughter is the shortest distance between two people."

9. Focus on what you can control: Concentrate your energy on the aspects of your life that you can influence, and let go of the things you cannot control. As the Serenity Prayer states, "Grant me the serenity to accept the things I cannot change, the courage to change the things I can, and the wisdom to know the difference."

10. Reflect on past successes: Take time to reflect on previous challenges you've overcome and the strengths that helped you persevere. As author and motivational speaker Jack Canfield says, "Everything you've ever been through can be of value if you choose to see it that way."

By incorporating these strategies and following the advice of industry experts, you can build mental resilience to navigate life's challenges better. Developing mental resilience enhances your mental health and empowers you to face adversity with courage and grace.

Soichiro Honda was born in a small village in Japan in 1906. From a young age, he developed a passion for machinery and automobiles. His father, a blacksmith who ran a bicycle repair shop, fueled this fascination. Despite limited resources and education, Honda's curiosity and drive to learn led him to experiment with engines and mechanical devices.

In his early twenties, Honda moved to Tokyo to work as an apprentice in an auto repair shop. He worked tirelessly to hone his skills and eventually returned to his hometown to start his auto repair business. However, his ambitions continued. He dreamt of designing and manufacturing his automobile parts.

During World War II, Honda's business was severely impacted. His factory was destroyed in a bombing raid, and he was forced to sell his remaining equipment to stay afloat. Despite this significant setback, Honda refused to let go of his dreams.

After the war, Honda started a new venture, manufacturing motorized bicycles. He created an engine that could be attached to a bike, and soon enough, his products gained popularity in post-war Japan. The success of these motorized bicycles laid the foundation for the Honda Motor Co., Ltd., established in 1948.

However, Honda's journey could have been smoother sailing. His first motorcycle, the Dream, was met with lukewarm reception due to its high price and noisy engine. Instead of giving up, Honda viewed this failure as an opportunity to learn and improve. He doubled down on research and development, eventually creating a more affordable and reliable motorcycle, the Super Cub.

The Super Cub became a resounding success, not only in Japan but also in markets around the world. This triumph marked the beginning of Honda's rise to prominence in the global automotive industry.

In the 1960s, Honda entered the automobile market, challenging established giants like Toyota and Nissan. His company's first car, the S500 sports car, was followed by the revolutionary N360, a compact car that catered to Japan's growing urban population.

Honda's success in the automotive industry can be attributed to his relentless pursuit of innovation and his refusal to accept failure as an outcome. He once said, "Success represents the one percent of your work which results from the ninety-nine percent that is called failure."

Throughout his life, Honda faced numerous personal and professional challenges and setbacks. He battled multiple health issues and even survived a near-fatal car accident. However, his mental resilience and unwavering determination allowed him to persevere and overcome these obstacles.

15.2 Strategies for Coping with Anxiety and Depression

Anxiety and depression are complex mental health issues arising from genetics, brain chemistry, personality traits, and life experiences. These conditions can significantly impact an individual's well-being, relationships, and overall quality of life. However, understanding the root causes and implementing effective strategies can lead to substantial improvements in managing anxiety and depression.

A significant cause of anxiety and depression is the ongoing experience of stress. Chronic stress can lead to a constant state of worry and fear, which can ultimately manifest as anxiety or depression. To combat stress-induced anxiety and depression, it is crucial to identify and address the sources of stress in one's life. This may involve setting boundaries, practicing stress-reduction techniques, or seeking professional help to develop healthier coping mechanisms.

Another contributing factor to anxiety and depression is a lack of social support. Feeling isolated and disconnected from others can exacerbate mental health issues. Building a strong social network of friends, family members, and supportive communities can make a significant difference in managing anxiety and depression. By fostering connections with others who understand and empathize with your experiences, you can create a support system that helps you through difficult times.

Genetics and brain chemistry also play a role in developing anxiety and depression. Some individuals may be more predisposed to these conditions due to their genetic makeup or imbalances in neurotransmitters. In such cases, consulting with mental health professionals and considering medication options may be an effective strategy to manage these conditions.

Moreover, negative thought patterns and cognitive distortions can contribute to anxiety and depression. Cognitive-behavioral therapy (CBT) is a proven technique to identify and challenge these unhelpful thought patterns. By working with a therapist or utilizing self-help resources, you can learn to reframe your thoughts and develop healthier, more constructive thought patterns.

Poor physical health can also contribute to anxiety and depression. Regular exercise, a balanced diet, and adequate sleep are essential for maintaining physical and mental health. By prioritizing self-care and engaging in activities that promote physical well-being, you can create a strong foundation for managing anxiety and depression.

Another coping strategy for anxiety and depression is cultivating a sense of purpose and meaning in life. Engaging in meaningful activities, pursuing personal goals, and contributing to the well-being of others can help shift focus away from negative thoughts and emotions. By aligning your life with your values and passions, you can foster a sense of fulfillment and resilience in the face of adversity.

Practicing mindfulness and meditation is another effective approach to managing anxiety and depression. By learning to focus on the present moment, you can develop greater awareness and acceptance of your thoughts and emotions, reducing the power they hold over you.

Additionally, creative expressions, such as art, writing, or music, can provide an outlet for emotions and a therapeutic tool for managing anxiety and depression. By engaging in creative activities, you can process and express your emotions constructively and healingly.

Developing a healthy balance between work and personal life is also essential. Overworking and neglecting self-care can contribute to anxiety and depression. You can create a more sustainable and fulfilling lifestyle by setting boundaries and prioritizing personal well-being.

Finally, remember that seeking professional help is always an option. Mental health professionals can provide valuable guidance, support, and treatment tailored to your needs. By reaching out for help, you can access resources and expertise to help you navigate the challenges of anxiety and depression.

In conclusion, understanding the causes of anxiety and depression and implementing effective strategies can significantly improve your ability to manage these conditions. Taking a proactive approach to your mental health can foster greater resilience, well-being, and overall quality of life.

Kevin Hines was born in San Francisco in 1981, and early in life, he faced numerous challenges, including trauma, abuse, and a tumultuous upbringing. At 17, Hines was diagnosed with bipolar disorder, and he struggled to manage the debilitating symptoms of anxiety and depression that came with it.

As Hines' mental health deteriorated, he found it increasingly difficult to cope with his emotions and thoughts. One fateful day in September 2000, at 19, Hines decided to end his life by jumping off the Golden Gate Bridge. Miraculously, he survived the fall, becoming one of the few individuals to have survived such an attempt.

The aftermath of his suicide attempt marked the beginning of a long and arduous journey to recovery. Hines realized he needed to control his life and mental health to ensure a better future. With unwavering determination and willpower, he began implementing various coping strategies to manage his anxiety and depression.

One key element of Hines' recovery was seeking professional help. He began working with therapists and psychiatrists, who helped him develop healthier thought patterns and coping mechanisms. This support network provided Hines with guidance and tools to navigate the challenges of living with bipolar disorder.

Another significant aspect of Hines' recovery was establishing a strong social support system. He connected with others who had experienced similar struggles and built a community that understood and empathized with his challenges. This support network proved invaluable in helping Hines overcome his anxiety and depression.

Hines also focused on his physical health, regularly exercising and maintaining a balanced diet. He recognized the strong link between physical and mental well-being and consciously prioritized his self-care. This holistic approach to wellness played a crucial role in Hines' recovery.

Furthermore, Hines found solace in mindfulness and meditation practices, which helped him stay grounded and present. By learning to manage his thoughts and emotions through mindfulness, Hines developed greater resilience and coping skills to deal with his anxiety and depression.

As Hines' mental health improved, he discovered a passion for helping others facing similar struggles. He began sharing his story publicly and became a mental health advocate, traveling the world as a motivational speaker. Hines' powerful message of hope and resilience has inspired countless individuals battling mental health issues.

In 2016, Hines' story was featured in the documentary film, "Suicide: The Ripple Effect," which raised awareness about mental health and suicide prevention. Through his advocacy work, Hines has touched the lives of millions, helping to break the stigma surrounding mental health and encouraging others to seek help.

By sharing his story, Hines provides hope to countless individuals worldwide who may be struggling with their mental health. He is a shining example of what can be achieved through determination, willpower, and effective strategies to overcome anxiety and depression.

15.3 The Role of Willpower in Addiction Recovery

The role of willpower in addiction recovery has been a significant interest within psychology. Researchers have conducted numerous studies to understand better how to harness willpower effectively to overcome addiction. One such study that provides valuable insights into the role of willpower and self-control in addiction recovery is a series of experiments led by psychologist Dr. Alan Marlatt.

Dr. Marlatt's research focused on relapse prevention, a cognitive-behavioral approach to helping individuals maintain long-term recovery from addiction. His experiments examined how individuals can utilize willpower and self-control techniques to resist the temptation to use drugs or alcohol when faced with high-risk situations or triggers.

In one of Dr. Marlatt's experiments, participants recovering from addiction were divided into two groups. One group received traditional treatment, primarily identifying and addressing the underlying issues contributing to their addiction. The other group received additional relapse prevention training, incorporating cognitive-behavioral strategies to enhance willpower and self-control.

The relapse prevention training included techniques such as identifying high-risk situations, developing coping strategies, and practicing mindfulness to help participants resist cravings and maintain their recovery. Participants were also taught how to recognize early warning signs of relapse and implement self-control strategies to prevent a full-blown relapse.

The experiment was designed to assess the effectiveness of these willpower-enhancing techniques in promoting long-term recovery from addiction. Participants were followed for one year, during which researchers monitored their progress and evaluated their ability to maintain sobriety.

At the end of the study, Dr. Marlatt and his team found that participants who had received the relapse prevention training, which focused on enhancing willpower and self-control, experienced significantly lower relapse rates than those who had received traditional treatment alone.

The results of this experiment highlight the importance of incorporating willpower-enhancing strategies into addiction recovery programs. By teaching individuals how to harness their willpower and develop self-control skills effectively, they are better equipped to resist cravings, manage triggers, and maintain long-term recovery.

This research also underscores the importance of a comprehensive approach to addiction recovery. While addressing the underlying issues contributing to addiction is essential, incorporating strategies to enhance willpower and self-control can significantly improve the likelihood of successful long-term recovery.

Furthermore, the findings of Dr. Marlatt's study have implications for the broader field of psychology, as they demonstrate the power of willpower and self-control in overcoming a range of challenges beyond addiction, such as managing stress, improving emotional regulation, and achieving personal goals.

In addiction recovery, stories of resilience and willpower can inspire hope and provide a valuable example for others struggling. One such story is that of Jodie Sweetin, an actress best known as Stephanie Tanner on the hit sitcom "Full House" and its sequel, "Fuller House." Sweetin's journey of overcoming addiction and her subsequent work as a recovery advocate has been widely reported in the news.

Jodie Sweetin's battle with addiction began at a young age. After the end of "Full House" in 1995, she struggled to cope with the pressures of growing up in the public eye. Sweetin began experimenting with alcohol and drugs, eventually developing a severe addiction to methamphetamine and other substances.

Sweetin struggled with her addiction for years, going through a series of rehab stints and relapses. In 2005, she hit rock bottom when she was hospitalized following a dangerous drug binge. At this moment, Sweetin realized she needed to make a drastic change in her life.

With unwavering determination and willpower, Sweetin embarked on a journey toward sobriety. She entered a rehabilitation program, committing herself fully to the recovery process. Sweetin's dedication to overcoming her addiction was evident in her willingness to confront the underlying issues that had fueled her substance abuse.

Throughout her recovery process, Sweetin employed various willpower-enhancing strategies, such as identifying triggers, developing healthy coping mechanisms, and practicing mindfulness. By harnessing her willpower and focusing on her goals, Sweetin could resist the temptation of relapse and maintain her sobriety.

Sweetin also recognized the importance of having a strong support system to aid her in her journey. She surrounded herself with friends, family, and fellow individuals in recovery who understood her challenges and provided encouragement during difficult moments. This support network played a crucial role in Sweetin's ability to maintain sobriety.

As Sweetin's recovery progressed, she found new ways to channel her energy and focus on positive pursuits. She began pursuing acting roles again and landed a part in the sequel to "Full House," "Fuller House," which premiered on Netflix in 2016. This new opportunity allowed Sweetin to reestablish her acting career and showcase her personal growth.

In addition to her acting work, Sweetin became a vocal advocate for addiction recovery. She began sharing her story publicly, speaking at events and conferences about her experiences with addiction and her journey toward sobriety. Sweetin's message of hope and resilience resonated with countless individuals facing similar struggles.

In 2009, Sweetin released a memoir, "UnSweetined," detailing her experiences with addiction and her path to recovery. The book provided a candid account of her life, offering valuable insights and lessons for others struggling with substance abuse.

Now let's put them together.

In the landscape of the human mind, willpower stands as a mighty mountain, casting its shadow over the vast terrain of our mental health. The peaks of this towering summit represent the various aspects of mental fortitude: developing mental resilience, coping with anxiety and depression, and overcoming addiction. When we harness the power of willpower to ascend these peaks, we find ourselves conquering the internal battles that once seemed impossible.

The climb to mental resilience is a steep and challenging ascent, requiring us to forge new paths and learn from those who have scaled the heights before us. As we embrace the wisdom of industry experts and apply their guidance to our own lives, we strengthen our resolve and develop the mental endurance needed to weather the storms of life. The summit of mental resilience rewards us with a panoramic view of our newfound strength, allowing us to face adversity with unwavering determination.

Descending into the valley of anxiety and depression, we encounter a labyrinth of shadows and fog. To navigate this treacherous terrain, we must rely on the compass of willpower, guiding us through the darkness with strategies and insights gleaned from those who have traversed the valley before. As we apply these lessons and forge our path forward, the fog dissipates, and the shadows recede, unveiling a newfound clarity and hope.

To conquer the formidable peak of addiction recovery, we must summon our inner strength and face the relentless winds that threaten to sweep us off our feet. Willpower serves as our anchor, securing us to the mountainside as we employ the techniques and guidance of experts who have helped others reach the summit. With each step, we push beyond our limits, inching closer to the top where freedom and self-mastery await.

The mountain range of willpower stretches across our mental health landscape, connecting the peaks of mental resilience, anxiety and depression management, and addiction recovery. By conquering these summits, we embrace the power to shape our destiny, surmount our challenges, and emerge victorious in our quest for inner peace and self-realization.

www.ingramcontent.com/pod-product-compliance
Lightning Source LLC
LaVergne TN
LVHW012046160826
845678LV00014B/2715

* 9 7 8 1 8 0 1 2 8 8 3 5 4 *